Cambridge Elements

Elements in Language and Power
edited by
Luis Javier Pentón Herrera
VIZJA University
Sender Dovchin
Curtin University

LANGUAGE AS POWER IN THE LANGUAGE TEACHER EDUCATION ECOSYSTEM

Jaber Kamali
Ibn Haldun University

Shaftesbury Road, Cambridge CB2 8EA, United Kingdom

One Liberty Plaza, 20th Floor, New York, NY 10006, USA

477 Williamstown Road, Port Melbourne, VIC 3207, Australia

314–321, 3rd Floor, Plot 3, Splendor Forum, Jasola District Centre,
New Delhi – 110025, India

Cambridge University Press is part of Cambridge University Press & Assessment,
a department of the University of Cambridge.

We share the University's mission to contribute to society through the pursuit of
education, learning and research at the highest international levels of excellence.

www.cambridge.org
Information on this title: www.cambridge.org/9781009733816

DOI: 10.1017/9781009733823

© Jaber Kamali 2026

This publication is in copyright. Subject to statutory exception and to the provisions
of relevant collective licensing agreements, no reproduction of any part may take
place without the written permission of Cambridge University Press & Assessment.

When citing this work, please include a reference to the DOI 10.1017/9781009733823

First published 2026

A catalogue record for this publication is available from the British Library

*A Cataloging-in-Publication data record for this Element is available from the Library
of Congress*

ISBN 978-1-009-73381-6 Hardback
ISBN 978-1-009-73380-9 Paperback
ISSN 2977-778X (online)
ISSN 2977-7771 (print)

Cambridge University Press & Assessment has no responsibility for the persistence
or accuracy of URLs for external or third-party internet websites referred to in this
publication and does not guarantee that any content on such websites is, or will remain,
accurate or appropriate.

For EU product safety concerns, contact us at Calle de José Abascal, 56, 1°, 28003
Madrid, Spain, or email eugpsr@cambridge.org

Language as Power in the Language Teacher Education Ecosystem

Elements in Language and Power

DOI: 10.1017/9781009733823
First published online: February 2026

Jaber Kamali
Ibn Haldun University

Author for correspondence: Jaber Kamali, jaber.kamali@ihu.edu.tr

Abstract: This Element aims to examine how language operates as power across the ecosystem of language teacher education (LTE). It maps how language-as-power (LaP) works at three layers: microsystem (teachers and classrooms), mesosystem (institutions), and macrosystem (socio-politics). Section 1 surveys LaP historically, tracing its historical evolution from Plato to contemporary theorists and showing how these ideas shape LTE. Building on this history, Sections 2–4 unpack LaP across ecological layers: microsystem, mesosystem, and macrosystem. Section 5 looks forward, analyzing AI's redistribution of power at each scale, and applying a 3Ps (possible, probable, and preferable) futurology to chart potential pathways. Anchored in experiences from the Global South, the Element argues that LaP in LTE needs awareness and action. It offers ideas on how to address these issues in LTE through solutions such as widening epistemic access, contesting monolingual norms, and institutionalizing dialogic, justice-oriented professionalism and trans-speakerism, to name a few.

Keywords: language-as-power, language teacher education, language teacher, language education, teacher education

© Jaber Kamali 2026
ISBNs: 9781009733816 (HB), 9781009733809 (PB), 9781009733823 (OC)
ISSNs: 2977-778X (online), 2977-7771 (print)

Contents

Preface	1
1 LaP and the Foundations of LTE	3
2 LaP in LTE Microsystem	16
3 LaP in LTE Mesosystem	29
4 LaP in LTE Macrosystem	41
5 Future Trajectories of LaP in the LTE Ecosystem	55
References	63

Preface

We live in a world of politics, and power determines every aspect of our lives. It is overly simplistic to think that our lives are apolitical and that we live without any influence of power. The role of power is evident in our personal, cultural, social, and even ideological decisions. Power has even influenced our tastes. Beauty now has different meanings and is different from what it was in old ages (perhaps Aphrodite, the ancient Greek goddess of love and beauty, would not be considered beautiful anymore if she lived today). Beauty operations have the same pattern these days because the standards of beauty have been defined by the elements of power. In sports, teams that receive strong support have more fans. Billions of dollars are spent on them, and no one has an issue with it. This is how power intentionally or unintentionally enters our lives. When it comes to education, it becomes even more important. Education is a place where you can be influenced by power and learn how to influence others through power. Within this, educating teachers regarding this is of utmost importance.

In my conversation with Luis (one of the editors of the series), we explored how one of these types of power, that is, language, has suppressed our feelings, our skills, and even our rights as teachers from the Global South and as individuals whose roots lie in that part of the world. That exchange became a turning point in my life. It was then that I resolved to write a Cambridge Element on this very issue, examining how linguistic and discursive power operates across, and manipulates, the multiple layers of the language teacher education (LTE) ecosystem in which we live and work. This personal and professional awakening naturally shaped the structure of this Element, a structure that itself evolved and transformed multiple times throughout the review process.

Before outlining this Element's structure, it is important to clarify the central perspective that informs its analysis. While the issues explored apply to LTE across languages, most examples come from English language teaching (ELT). This reflects my professional background and ELT's dominance in empirical research, which shapes how LTE is framed. Such prominence can also reinforce ideological hierarchies, making ELT a revealing and critical lens for examining language as power (LaP) within the LTE ecosystem.

With this point clarified, the opening section, Section 1, sets the stage by offering a historical analysis of how language operates as power and how this idea has shaped LTE. I trace a lineage from classical thought, such as Plato's concerns with rhetoric, persuasion, and civic governance, to contemporary theorists such as Foucault, who reconceptualizes power as dispersed through discourse, and Phillipson, who foregrounds linguistic imperialism. By following this chronological arc, the section shows how these paradigms have informed LTE's norms, curricula, and evaluative practices. This historical framing prepares the ground for later sections that examine how these inherited ideas surface in teachers and classrooms (i.e., microsystem), in institutional routines like observation and assessment (i.e., mesosystem), and across broader political-economic forces (i.e., macrosystem).

Section 2 examines the microsystem (i.e., teachers and classrooms) where LaP is most immediate. It explores how teacher identity, stance, and everyday classroom talk shape authority, participation, and epistemic access. It also considers micro-resistance, such as silence, humor, and translanguaging, as agentive responses that reconfigure inclusion and voice. The section closes by drawing broad implications for LTE design that cultivate reflexivity, discourse awareness, and equitable interactional norms.

Section 3 shifts to the mesosystem, dealing with institutions or Language Teaching Organizations (LTOs), where institutional routines translate ideology into practice. It examines how Professional Development (PD) infrastructures, policies, handbooks, and observation and feedback cycles shape who is authorized to speak, what counts as "good" language, and how compliance is produced. The section also outlines broad strategies for contesting hegemony and enabling teacher agency within institutional constraints.

Section 4 situates LaP in the macrosystem: The sociopolitical field shaping LTE. It interrogates standard language ideology (SLI) and native-speakerism; traces colonial political economy in Global South LTE; examines how linguistic capital, accreditation, and market logics stratify opportunities; and advances counter-moves that decenter monolingual ownership and recenter multilingualism. The section concludes with policy-level recommendations to disrupt structural inequities across funding, standards, and accountability regimes.

Section 5 looks ahead, mapping trajectories for LaP in LTE. It first examines artificial intelligence (AI)'s reconfiguration of power at micro (classroom and teacher identity), meso (LTO governance, assessment, PD), and macro (standards, markets, geopolitics) scales, surfacing risks and redistributive potentials. It then applies a 3Ps (possible, probable, and preferable) futurology lens to sketch scenarios, confront path dependencies, and argue for design choices that steer LTE toward equitable, multilingual, teacher-empowering futures.

In this Element, I argue that LTE is a continual negotiation of legitimacy, voice, and value. Across classrooms, institutions, and sociopolitical orders, I trace how routines, rubrics, markets, and myths authorize some ways of speaking while marginalizing others, and how teachers and learners carve out agency through reflective practice, micro-resistance, and multilingual design. Looking ahead, AI intensifies these stakes, making our futures not just foreseeable but choosable. Preferably, futures will require naming power, widening access to epistemic resources, and institutionalizing dialogue that is accountable to justice, not just efficiency. Neutrality is not an option; it simply preserves existing hierarchies. Borrowing the words of Szymborska (1995),

> I believe Apolitical *LTE* is also political . . .

1 LaP and the Foundations of LTE

1.1 Introducing Language and Power in the LTE Ecosystem

LTE comprises three components, within which language and power are inseparable and deeply intertwined concepts. The first component, language, far from being a neutral conduit for communication, operates as a powerful social tool that constructs and maintains relationships of dominance and resistance. Scholars have argued this for a long time in the literature (e.g., Bourdieu, 1991; Fairclough, 2013). The second component of LTE, teachers, wields power through their use of language, as they shape learners' identities, mediate access to linguistic and cultural capital, and reinforce or challenge ideologies within educational contexts (Diaz et al., 2016; Harmon & Wilson, 2012). Finally, education as the third component in LTE is inherently linked to power, as it involves the transmission of language norms, values, and ideologies that can either sustain or disrupt existing social hierarchies and cultural assumptions (e.g., see *Power and Education*, a journal entirely dedicated to exploring the interrelation of power and education). This interplay shapes the entire LTE ecosystem, which includes micro-, meso-, and macro-layers encompassing, inter alia, institutions, teacher education programs, PD activities, certification bodies, classroom interactions, and the sociocultural realities teachers experience.

The role of language and power plays a pivotal role in the LTE scholarship because it helps future educators critically examine how schools function as key sites where dominant ideologies are enforced (McKinney, 2016). Educational institutions promote an "ideal standard language" that excludes nonstandard, vernacular, or regionally marked varieties (Bourdieu, 1991; Lippi-Green, 1997). Although these instructional establishments claim to support equality and offer all students the same opportunities, in practice, they often marginalize linguistic and cultural diversity (Heller & Martin-Jones, 2001; Martín Rojo, 2010, 2013). The LTE has the potential to educate teachers on recognizing how power is exercised and negotiated via language through processes such as classroom practices that require students to use a specific variety, correct nonstandard usage, or discourage home languages (Pentón Herrera & Martínez-Alba,

2022). By raising awareness of these mechanisms, LTE has the potential to empower teachers to reflect on their own roles in either reinforcing or challenging linguistic hierarchies in educational settings (Hawkins & Norton, 2009; Johnson & Golombek, 2020).

The teaching and learning of language inherently involve assumptions about which languages, dialects, accents, and varieties are desirable or legitimate, which leads to a fundamental question: "How can one promote a common language for the community while supporting equal rights for all community languages at the same time?" (Seidlhofer et al., 2006, p. 24). These dilemmas reflect broader social power relation complexities, mostly privileging some ways of speaking and devaluing others. For example, many LTE programs emphasize standard varieties of English, often those spoken in Britain or the United States, positioning them as the *correct* or *ideal* forms by setting prerequisite standards for joining the teacher training courses (Dovchin, 2020). This standardization has consequences for teachers' self-perceptions and for the students they will eventually teach (Salton, 2019).

Linguistic power can also manifest in LTE through the institutionalization of certain linguistic norms and practices (Hilferty, 2008). Accreditation processes, assessment criteria, and teacher recruitment policies often reproduce dominant ideologies such as native speakerism (Daoud & Kasztalska, 2025): The belief that only those who speak a language *natively* are qualified to teach it. Such ideologies create hierarchies that marginalize non-native teachers, multilingual practices, and alternative pedagogies. I will elaborate on this more in Section 2.

To understand the power dynamics in LTE, it is crucial to recognize that LTE is embedded in complex social, political, and historical contexts (Johnson, 2016). The language norms upheld in teacher education, albeit increasingly challenged by heightened critical awareness and more inclusive approaches, go beyond mere pedagogical choices, reflecting historical legacies of colonialism, globalization, and cultural dominance. This section explores foundational philosophical and theoretical perspectives on language and power, tracing their evolution to contemporary theoretical frameworks that challenge and complicate dominant narratives within LTE.

1.1.1 Layers and Stakeholders of LTE Ecosystem

Although various studies have proposed different typologies of ecological layers (Bronfenbrenner, 1979, 1993; van Lier, 2004), this Element adopts the most widely recognized and commonly used model, which comprises three core levels: the microsystem, mesosystem, and macrosystem. This simplification allows for a more focused analysis of the immediate, relational, and

Language as Power in the Language Teacher Education Ecosystem 5

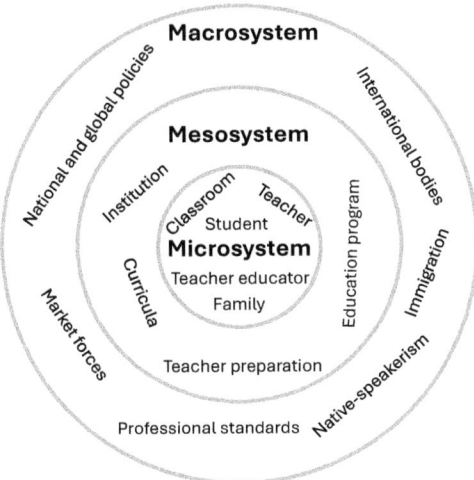

Figure 1 Schematic representation of the ecological layers of LTE

broader sociocultural influences on the phenomenon under investigation. The LTE ecosystem encompasses a broad network of actors and layers, each contributing to the complex interplay of language and power (see Figure 1). Understanding these layers helps clarify how power circulates and is contested within LTE.

- **Microsystem:** At this level, the classroom and teacher-student interactions are milieus where power dynamics are enacted, practiced, and negotiated daily. Individuals, such as teacher educators and teachers, play a central role in shaping and reshaping these power dynamics. These microlevel engagements become critical sites for cultivating awareness of linguistic diversity, equity, and inclusion
- **Mesosystem:** At this level, institutions such as universities, LTOs, teacher training colleges, and language schools establish curricula, accredit programs, and set the standards for teacher preparation. Institutional priorities often reflect national language ideologies and international trends, which can privilege certain linguistic and pedagogical norms over others.
- **Macrosystem:** At this level, national and global policies on language education, immigration, and professional standards influence LTE. International bodies and market forces also shape the demand for certain languages and the models of teacher education that gain prestige and credibility worldwide.

Understanding language and power in the LTE ecosystem invites a critical interrogation of whose knowledge, language, and identity are valued and how teacher education can be reimagined to foster linguistic equity and social transformation.

1.1.2 Language as a Social Practice

Language is more than a system of signs or a tool for communication; it is a social practice embedded with meanings, values, and ideological forces (Woolard, 2020). Language mediates our experiences and relationships, shapes identities, and organizes social realities (Nunan & Choi, 2010). In the LTE ecosystem, the complex network of institutions, individuals, policies, curricula, and practices involved in preparing language teachers, language is both the content to be taught and the means through which teaching occurs.

In sociolinguistic terms, language is inseparable from culture, identity, and power (Norton, 1997). It functions as a marker of social membership, distinguishing groups and individuals by ethnicity, class, gender, nationality, and other categories. The varieties of language, accents, and dialects people use carry social significance and status, serving as more than neutral forms of expression (Morgan, 1997). For example, in discussing the role of pronunciation and intonation in practicing power, Morgan (1997) argued that, "What stands out ... is how the foregrounding of social power and identity issues seemed to facilitate greater comprehension of sentence level stress and intonation as strategic resources for (re)defining social relationships" (p. 431).

Language's role in LTE thus involves transmitting and sometimes challenging these sociocultural meanings and power dynamics. Language teachers are trained in linguistic forms and teaching methodologies while also engaging with and navigating the social dimensions of language use (Korthagen, 2017). Teachers' socialization into certain linguistic norms (Mökkönen, 2012), their perceptions of their own and their students' language identities (Kayi-Aydar, 2019), and the pedagogical practices they enact (Kamali, 2024) are all deeply shaped by the power relations embedded in language.

1.1.3 Defining LaP in LTE

In this Element, I define LaP in the LTE ecosystem as the capacity to influence, control, and shape teacher knowledge, teacher identities, pedagogical practices, and institutional policies informed by the use of language. It operates at multiple layers, from using language in interpersonal interactions in the classroom to using it in institutional regulations and global ideologies.

Language as Power in the Language Teacher Education Ecosystem

LaP can be understood through Foucault's (1980) notion of power/knowledge, which frames power as productive rather than purely repressive; it generates knowledge, truths, and norms that shape and regulate behavior (Seidman & Alexander, 2020). Power circulates through discourses, which are structured ways of speaking and thinking that define what is considered legitimate knowledge and practice (Foucault, 1980).

In LTE, LaP manifests in decisions about what counts as *correct* language, whose linguistic knowledge is valued, and what pedagogical approaches to teach them are deemed effective. For instance, the privileging of native speaker norms and standard language ideologies reflects and reproduces power asymmetries between native and non-native teachers, between teachers from dominant and marginalized linguistic groups, and between global North and South contexts (Phillipson, 1992).

Power also operates through institutional mechanisms such as teacher certification processes and accreditation standards (Barduhn & Johnson, 2009), curriculum design (Paechter, 2000), and assessment tools (Tan, 2012). These mechanisms regulate who can become a language teacher, what competencies they must demonstrate, and how their professional identities are shaped and maintained. Such regulation often mirrors broader social hierarchies and can reinforce inequities based on race, class, nationality, and language.

1.2 Historical and Theoretical Perspectives of LaP in LTE

Language has long been intertwined with power, authority, and social control (Fairclough, 2013). In LTE, understanding the historical and global dimensions of linguistic authority is crucial for unpacking how power relations are embedded and reproduced in language education. This section traces the philosophical and historical roots of language and authority, beginning with foundational thinkers such as Plato, moving through the modern analyses of Michel Foucault, Paulo Freire, and others, and culminating in critical, poststructuralist, and decolonial theories (See Table 1). These perspectives reveal how LTE both reflects and challenges dominant linguistic ideologies that shape access, legitimacy, and identity within the global language education landscape.

1.2.1 Plato

The philosophical engagement with language as a vehicle of power and knowledge can be traced back to the classical thinker, Plato. For Plato, language served as more than a tool for communication; it was a medium intimately linked to ethics, truth, and governance. In dialogues such as *Cratylus* and *The*

Table 1 Summary of historical and theoretical perspectives of language power in LTE

Historical /theoretical perspective	Key thinkers	Main concepts	Implications for LTE
Early foundations	Plato	Language as a moral-philosophical tool; ethics, truth, and rhetoric; language as social control	Frames language use in education in general and LTE in particular as ethically charged; foundational for understanding language as a tool of influence
Discourse and power/ knowledge	Foucault	Discourse as productive of knowledge, identities, and truths; power/knowledge dynamic	Conceptualizes LTE as being shaped by institutional discourses (e.g., native speaker norms); posits that power is embedded in what is taught and legitimized
Colonial legacy	Phillipson	Linguistic imperialism; colonial imposition of language; normalization of colonial languages in education	Explains global linguistic hierarchies; critiques LTE's role in reinforcing colonial legacies and standard language ideologies
Language as praxis	Freire	Language as dialogic and reflective action (praxis); critical consciousness; pedagogy to democratize	Promotes bottom-up, socially just LTE; highlights the political nature of language education and the need to empower teachers/ learners
Linguistic capital	Bourdieu	Language as symbolic and cultural capital; habitus; social stratification	Posits that LTE reproduces linguistic hierarchies; urges critical awareness of how language privileges operate and are internalized

Postmethod pedagogy	Kumaravadivelu	Rejection of prescriptive methods; teacher autonomy; context-sensitive pedagogy	Encourages adaptive, critically reflective LTE; decentralizes authority from theory to teacher practice
Decolonial epistemologies	Mignolo	Coloniality of knowledge; delinking from Western paradigms; epistemic diversity	Urges LTE to integrate indigenous/local knowledges; promotes pluriversal approaches and decolonial alternatives
Contemporary critical approaches	Fairclough, Pennycook, Canagarajah	Critical discourse analysis; narrative inquiry; translingualism; identity and power; anti-authoritarianism	Consider LTE a space for ideological critique and teacher identity negotiation; advocates for inclusive, critical, and pluralistic practices

Republic, Plato considered the relationship between words, meaning, and reality, emphasizing the moral responsibilities tied to language use.

Plato's ethical view of language foregrounds the idea that language can either illuminate truth or mislead, thereby influencing social order and justice. His skepticism about the persuasive power of rhetoric, especially when divorced from truth, foreshadows later concerns about how language functions in maintaining or challenging authority. This is evident in *Gorgias*, where rhetoric is described as "the art of ruling the minds of men" (Plato, trans. 2004, *Gorgias*, 452e), highlighting Plato's unease with language used as a tool for domination rather than dialogue. Although Plato's reflections were primarily philosophical and ethical, they set the stage for understanding language as deeply embedded in power relations, which is crucial for modern explorations of linguistic authority. Consequently, in LTE, classroom discourse, curricular framing, and assessment talk should be treated as ethical acts. LTE must cultivate truth-seeking rhetoric over mere persuasion and equip teachers to interrogate how language distributes authority.

1.2.2 Foucault

Fast-forwarding to the twentieth century, Michel Foucault's theories radically reshaped how we think about language, power, and knowledge. Foucault rejected the notion of language as a transparent medium and instead proposed the concept of discourse: systems of knowledge, practices, and institutions that produce and regulate what can be said, thought, and known.

For Foucault, discourse is inseparable from power. He contends, "Power produces; it produces reality; it produces domains of objects and rituals of truth. The individual and the knowledge that may be gained of him belong to this production" (Foucault, 1979, p. 194). It creates subjects, realities, and truths. Language and discourse shape social identities and knowledge regimes, determining who can speak, what counts as legitimate knowledge, and how truth is constructed. This insight is profoundly relevant for LTE, as it is itself a site where discourses about language proficiency, native speaker norms, and pedagogical approaches are institutionalized and disseminated.

Foucault's notion of power/knowledge reveals that linguistic authority emerges from and is sustained within the very structures of knowledge production and educational practice, rather than being solely imposed from above. For example, the privileging of *standard English* or *native speaker* models is not merely a matter of linguistic preference but a reflection of discursive formations that sustain power relations.

1.2.3 Philipson

The global landscape of language education, in particular LTE, is intertwined with the legacy of European colonialism (Macedo, 2019) when we consider languages such as English, French, Spanish, and Portuguese as the languages of colonizers. Languages are not racist per se (Pentón Herrera, 2022), but colonial powers imposed their languages as instruments of control, governance, and cultural domination. The educational systems established during colonial rule aimed to create intermediaries, often local elites fluent in the colonizer's language, to administer and legitimize colonial authority (Watson, 1992). For example, in the African context, this colonization was so deep-rooted that decolonization still left as "one of the biggest challenges not only in terms of the curriculum, teaching strategies, and textbooks, but also in terms of the democratization of knowledge and the regeneration, evaluation, and adaptation of old epistemologies to suit new post-colonial realities" (Emeagwali et al., 2014, p. 2).

This historical context is essential to understanding contemporary linguistic authority within LTE. The dominance of English as a global lingua franca, as an example, is deeply rooted in these colonial histories, even as English has evolved into a language of globalization and international communication. The colonial legacy persists in the valorization of native speaker norms, standard language ideologies, and the marginalization of local and indigenous languages (McKinney, 2016).

The process of linguistic imperialism (Phillipson, 1992) highlights how language teaching can perpetuate colonial power structures by maintaining asymmetries in whose language, culture, and knowledge are considered authoritative. As Phillipson (2013) asserted, the factors contributing to the increased use of English in Europe are structural and ideological, which can also be generalized to other colonial languages. Colonialingualism (Meighan, 2022) further underscores how educational systems normalize the dominance of colonial languages, embedding them as the default modes of expression and thought while marginalizing local and indigenous linguistic practices. LTE programs often reproduce these hierarchies by privileging native-speaker teachers and monolingual competencies, reinforcing colonial patterns of linguistic authority.

1.2.4 Freire

The critical pedagogical tradition, with Freire as a seminal figure (Freire, 2000/1970), offers a counterpoint to these colonial and institutional power structures by framing language education as a site of liberation and social transformation.

Freire's work emphasizes language as praxis: A reflective and dialogic process through which individuals become conscious of their social conditions and challenge oppression.

Freire's concept of critical consciousness (Freire, 2000/1970) has profoundly influenced Critical LTE, encouraging educators and teachers to recognize how language teaching is never neutral but is implicated in systems of power. Language educators are called to adopt a critical stance, fighting for politically sound versions of language teaching and LTE, fostering learners' agency, and resisting dominant linguistic ideologies that perpetuate inequality. The idea, which was asserted by various scholars (see Hawkins & Norton, 2009; Kamali, 2025)

Freirean principles advocate for teacher education that is contextually grounded, participatory, and socially just. The one that prioritizes a problem-posing approach in education, where everybody has a voice. This involves raising awareness about linguistic imperialism, encouraging multilingualism, and promoting pedagogies that affirm teachers' and learners' identities and cultural backgrounds rather than assimilating them into dominant language norms.

1.2.5 Bourdieu

Bourdieu's sociological theory of language and symbolic power offers a key analytic tool for understanding how linguistic authority functions within social stratification. Bourdieu conceptualizes language as a form of cultural capital, which is a resource that can be exchanged, accumulated, and converted into social power (Bourdieu, 1991). Given that the LTE context functions as a microcosm of broader society, Bourdieu's framework is equally applicable, illuminating how linguistic capital operates within its hierarchical structures.

In this framework, linguistic competence in a *legitimate* language variety (often the standard or prestige dialect) confers symbolic power, enabling access to educational and economic opportunities. This concept illuminates why certain language varieties or even stakeholders (e.g., policy makers or teacher educators) are privileged in LTE and why linguistic inequalities persist.

Bourdieu's notion of habitus, the internalized dispositions shaped by social conditions, helps explain how teachers and learners often unconsciously reproduce dominant language ideologies, accepting certain norms as natural or legitimate through marginalization or self-marginalization (Philipson, 1992). For example, the widespread acceptance of native speakerism is often unexamined because it is embedded in teachers' habitus and institutional practices.

Understanding LTE through Bourdieu's lens underscores the need for teacher education to disrupt these power relations by validating diverse linguistic repertoires and promoting critical awareness of the social functions of language.

1.2.6 Kumaravadivelu

Building on critical and poststructuralist theories, Kumaravadivelu (1994) introduces the concept of postmethod pedagogy, which calls for LTE that transcends prescriptive, one-size-fits-all methods (Kumaravadivelu, 2012). He emphasizes context-sensitive, teacher-empowering approaches that "celebrate difference, challenge hegemonies, and seek alternative forms of expression and interpretation" (Kumaravadivelu, 2012, p. 5).

Kumaravadivelu critiques the universalizing tendencies of dominant language teaching methods and underscores the importance of teacher autonomy, reflection, and critical engagement with language ideologies. His framework encourages LTE to move beyond replicating dominant linguistic norms and to cultivate teachers who can adapt practices to diverse sociocultural contexts. This approach resonates with broader critical and poststructuralist commitments to challenging power by decentralizing authority from institutions to teachers and learners themselves.

1.2.7 Mignolo

Mignolo (2012) provides a critical decolonial perspective that highlights the coloniality of knowledge and power: The persistence of colonial structures in contemporary global knowledge systems, including language education. Mignolo calls for delinking from Western epistemologies that dominate global educational paradigms and for embracing epistemic diversity. This can be practiced by decentralizing native accents and authorities, for example.

In the context of LTE, Mignolo's decolonial thought challenges the hegemony of Western language teaching paradigms and advocates for integrating indigenous and local knowledges and languages into teacher education, the trends which are celebrated with concepts such as translanguaging or teacher identities and agencies. This approach seeks to decenter Western language and culture and foster linguistic and cultural multilingualism as foundations for equitable and just language education.

Decolonial LTE thus becomes a project of resistance against linguistic imperialism, aiming to empower marginalized voices and transform the politics of language education on a global scale.

1.2.8 Contemporary Approaches to LTE from the LaP Perspective

Except for these well-known thinkers who argued the role of LaP in a general sense, there are other scholars who brought these concepts specifically into linguistics, applied linguistics, and LTE. One of these attempts was made by

Fairclough (1995), who claimed that "it is mainly in discourse that consent is achieved, ideologies are transmitted, and practices, meanings, values, and identities are taught and learnt" (p. 219). His Critical Discourse Analysis framework situates language as a social practice embedded in power relations, making it a central tool for examining inequality in educational settings.

In critical applied linguistics, Pennycook (2001) argued for " ... the importance of relating micro relations of applied linguistics to macro relations of society" (p. 2). He emphasized the importance of contextualizing language practices within larger sociopolitical structures, challenging the apolitical stance of traditional applied linguistics and advocating for a more reflexive, political orientation to language teaching and learning.

In conceptualizing critical LTE, Hawkins and Norton (2009) argued that a critical approach is responsive, dialogic, and reflexive, centering the voices and lived experiences of teachers, particularly those working in marginalized or multilingual contexts. Their work demonstrates how teachers' investments in language learning and their imagined identities are shaped by access to power, recognition, and participation in broader ideological communities.

Barkhuizen (2017), in conceptualizing narrative inquiry, emphasized that language, power, and teacher identity are deeply interconnected. He suggested that language use and the way teachers position themselves within various social and institutional contexts would influence their sense of professional identity. Power dynamics in interaction, such as those with colleagues, students, or within institutional structures, affect how teachers perceive themselves and how they are perceived by others. By analyzing narratives and stories, teachers can become more aware of how language contributes to these power relations, which in turn shape their identities and their capacity to negotiate their roles effectively within the educational setting.

Canagarajah's (1999, 2002) work in postcolonial applied linguistics exposed the hegemonic role of language in maintaining unequal power structures globally. In *Resisting Linguistic Imperialism*, he highlighted how teachers and learners in peripheral communities resist dominant ideologies through localized, negotiated practices. He later argued for translingual pedagogies that recognize multilingual competence as a resource rather than a deficit. In a related postcolonial register, Bhabha (1994) foregrounds how power and identity are historically conditioned and continuously negotiated, a view that encourages LTE to attend closely to how institutional discourses position teachers and how teachers respond within those conditions.

A critical voice against the ideological neutrality of language teaching, Kubota (1999, 2009) explored how racism, native-speakerism, and neoliberalism shape language education policies and teacher identities. She critiqued the hidden ideologies embedded in seemingly apolitical teaching methods, calling for a critical and socially aware teacher education that exposes and challenges linguistic inequalities.

Finally, I, elsewhere, conceptualized Anti-Machiavellian LTE (Kamali, 2025) as another liberal approach that seeks to liberate LTE from a top-down, fear-driven model, where language is used to impose authority and discourage critical engagement. I argued for a teacher education framework rooted in ethical responsibility, dialogic inquiry, and mutual trust, rejecting authoritarian approaches that suppress teachers' voices and reflection.

1.2.9 Applying Theoretical Approaches across LTE Ecosystem Layers

While these advancements and frameworks differ in emphasis and methodology, they share common goals of uncovering power relations and promoting social justice in LTE. Each contributes to the understanding of language and power at different layers of the LTE ecosystem and in complementary ways.

- **Microsystem:** Poststructuralist perspectives illuminate how power circulates through discourse between teachers and learners, shaping their identity formation and classroom dynamics. Critical LTE (e.g., Freire, 2000; Hawkins & Norton, 2009; Kamali, 2025) emphasizes the importance of creating pedagogical spaces that challenge dominant ideologies and empower diverse linguistic identities.
- **Mesosystem:** Universities and teacher training programs enact policies and curricula that mediate dominant discourses about language and teaching. Poststructuralist insights (Foucault, 1980; Kumaravadivelu, 2012) reveal how institutional discourses shape teachers' and teacher educators' identities and practices, while critical approaches critique accreditation regimes that marginalize multilingual pedagogies.
- **Macrosystem:** Critical and decolonial theories (e.g., Freire, 2000; Mignolo, 2012) expose how language policies and teacher certification standards reflect neoliberal market logics and colonial legacies. For example, global language teaching standards often prioritize native speaker norms, affecting teacher mobility and employment opportunities worldwide.

Together, these historical theoretical perspectives enable a multilayered analysis of LTE as an ecosystem where language and power intersect dynamically. They encourage researchers, policymakers, and practitioners to adopt a critical, reflexive, and transformative stance that acknowledges the complexity of power and the potential for resistance and change.

1.2.10 Conclusion

This historical and global overview reveals how LTE is profoundly shaped by philosophical reflections, institutional power structures, colonial legacies, and evolving critical theories. From Plato's ethical concerns to contemporary critical critiques, these perspectives illuminate the complex ways linguistic power operates within LTE.

Recognizing these historical roots and global language power dynamics equips language teachers, teacher educators, and policymakers with the critical tools to challenge dominant linguistic ideologies, promote social justice, and reimagine LTE as a transformative ecosystem. This involves embracing linguistic diversity, questioning normative standards, addressing issues of ownership and inequality, exploring the interplay between language and teacher identity, critically examining pedagogical and institutional discourses, and reimagining power relations in LTE through a lens of linguistic justice, especially in the context of emerging technologies like AI. In the next sections, I will discuss these aspects in turn.

2 LaP in LTE Microsystem

2.1 Language Power and the Person of the Teacher

The dichotomy of theory and practice in LTE has been attacked by different scholars. For example, Korthagen (2017) suggested that this dichotomy should be developed into a triangle whose vertices are theory, practice, and the person of the teacher. The last element is what needs more attention. The person of the teacher is made up of the teacher's mission, identity, beliefs, competencies, behavior, and environment, each embedded in layers like an onion (Korthagen, 2004). In this domain, language acts as a powerful tool as identified by Holzscheiter (2005) in three dimensions: Power in discourse, which involves struggles over meaning and control of interactional norms (e.g., who speaks, when, and how); power over discourse, referring to access which means who is visible or heard in public arenas; and power of discourse, the influence of deep, taken-for-granted language structures that shape thought and behavior over time. These three forms of power reveal the ways in which language, as a force, actively shapes teachers and their social order.

Reflecting on my own teaching and research journey, I've seen firsthand how language enacts power in subtle yet profound ways. *Power in discourse* was evident in my early years as a classroom teacher. During discussions, I unconsciously dominated the classroom talk, which refers to the spoken interaction between teachers and students during lessons (Alexander, 2017), deciding who spoke and how long, often correcting students mid-sentence. I believed that in this way I could impress my students. However, my control over interactional norms silenced their voices, even when they had valuable insights. *Power over discourse* became clear when I submitted my first research article on Iranian teachers' identity to an international journal. Despite its relevance, the paper was rejected with the comment, "not suitable for our readership." I realized that access to global academic spaces depends not only on quality but also on whose knowledge is deemed legitimate. The *power of discourse* appeared in my use of terms like "native-like pronunciation" in the placement tests for LTE programs. I never questioned this until much later in my career. This discourse shaped my expectations and preservice teachers' self-worth, reinforcing native-speakerism. Over time, I shifted toward promoting intelligibility and valuing multilingual identities.

A very relevant concept to language power and the person of the teacher is voice. Voice is about the individual behind the language, that is, how learners make personal choices to express themselves. Voice captures the personal side of language use (Kramsch, 2003). Teachers choose words, accents, and styles that reflect the identities they want to show or invest in (Baratta, 2018; Fairclough, 2003). This process involves picking up language from others and making it their own, shaping their distinct voice over time (Bakhtin, 1981; Canagarajah, 2013). Against this background, voice reveals how teachers' identities and investments come alive within social settings.

Power (such as discursive power) and the voice of language teachers are two important factors in language teacher identity (LTI), which is a cornerstone of the person of the teacher (Fairley, 2025). Power defines who belongs and who is excluded from a social milieu and shapes perceptions of similarity and difference. These distinctions often carry ideological implications and influence how people are categorized and valued. To look at it from Gee's lens (Gee, 2000), power is evident in four dimensions for identity, including Nature or N-identities, Institution or I-identities, Discourse or D-identities, and Affinity or A-identities. In N-identity, power reveals itself as an innate property of a teacher who is authoritarian. In I-identity, power is practiced through institutional levels, while higher positions, like supervisors, can impose ideas. The role of power in LTI is more evident in D-identity, which deals with "the ways one is recognized as a certain kind of person through discourse and discursive practices" (Nazari, 2025, p. 4).

Gee (2000) illustrates how identity is socially constructed by describing a friend seen as charismatic, not because of any inherent trait or institutional label, but because others treat and talk to her as such. This is in line with his concept of D-identities, which can be ascribed by others or actively shaped by individuals seeking recognition. Importantly, this process reveals how language, power, and identity are intertwined: The ways we speak, are spoken about, and position ourselves all shape how identities are formed and validated. Therefore, identity develops through interaction, shaped by discourse and the power dynamics embedded within it. A-identity which is "what people in the group share, and must share to constitute an affinity group, *is allegiance to, access to, and participation in specific practices* that provide each of the group's members the requisite experiences" (p. 105, original emphasis), also deals with power in LTI where the role of people in their affinity groups is defined by the inherent power.

Research on LTI has shown that although the process of identity construction is social (discursive), it is also deeply emotional (e.g., Dovchin et al., 2025; Kamali & Nazari, 2025; Pentón Herrera, 2024). For language teachers, being seen, heard, and taken seriously is important at both professional and personal levels (Pennington & Richards, 2016). When others acknowledge their voice and affirm who they are, it can build confidence and a sense of belonging; but when they are silenced, overlooked, or misrepresented, it can leave them feeling exposed, uncertain, and emotionally vulnerable (Gee, 2000; Nazari, 2025). Teaching, after all, is not just about delivering content but about bringing the self into the classroom. And when that self is shaped or constrained by how others speak about us, or whether we are granted legitimacy, the emotional toll can be significant.

2.2 Teacher and Classroom

First, let's explore why this discussion is relevant in this Element. Teachers might fall victim to power, but they are also its agents (consciously or unconsciously) through their interactional choices in the classroom. By analyzing moments of teacher talk, silence, and student participation, authority can be negotiated, reinforced, or resisted at the micro level. Fitzclarence and Giroux (1984) describe power in education as a spectrum from high-power to low-power settings. In the former, teachers define valid knowledge. In the latter, learners shape their own learning values. Freire (2000/1970) adds that teachers play a key role in legitimizing knowledge. He highlights how power shapes educational experiences and student agency. The manifestation of power in classroom talk can be found in authoritative and dialogic classroom discourse. In the authoritative one, there is only a single voice which is heard, accepted, or appreciated (the voice of the teacher) (Bakhtin, 1981). However, in the dialogic one, discussion and dialogue among all members of the classroom (teacher and students) are appreciated (Kim & Wilkinson, 2019). Dialogic teaching, therefore, has the following characteristics (Alexander, 2017, p. 28):

- Collective: Teachers and [students] address learning tasks together, whether as a group or as a class, rather than in isolation;
- Reciprocal: Teachers and [students] listen to each other, share ideas and consider alternative viewpoints;
- Supportive: [Students] articulate their ideas freely, without fear of embarrassment over "wrong" answers; and they help each other to reach common understandings;
- Cumulative: Teachers and [students] build on their own and each other's ideas and chain them into coherent lines of thinking and enquiry;
- Purposeful: Teachers plan and facilitate dialogic teaching with particular educational goals in view.

The initial three principles (i.e., collective, reciprocal, and supportive) lay the foundation for a collaborative classroom environment that fosters productive learning talk, while the remaining two focus specifically on the substance and quality of that talk (Alexander, 2017). There are a number of scholars who support dialogic pedagogy, including Freire (the first to articulate the term, to my knowledge), Burbules (1993), Nystrand (1997), Resnick (1999), Wells (1999), Wegerif (2011), and Alexander (2017), to name a few (for a complete list see Kim & Wilkinson, 2019). For example, Freire asserted that this concept required "the absence of authoritarianism" (Shor & Freire, 1987, p. 16), emphasizing the opposite nature of dialogic discourse with its authoritative counterpart, especially regarding the discursive power.

To clarify the discussion so far, the following section presents two excerpts from my doctoral research on interactional competence, illustrating instances of both dialogic and authoritative discourse in language teachers' talk.

01　**Teacher (T):**　Okay, listen carefully. When you report what someone says, the verb tense usually changes. For example, *He says, "I am tired"* becomes *He said he was tired.* Do you understand?

02	**Student (S)**:	Umm . . . why do we change the tense?
03	T:	Because that's the rule. It's how English works. You should just remember that. Let's move on. What's the reported form of *She says, "I like pizza"*?
04	S:	She said she liked pizza?
05	T:	Yes. That's the right form. Just follow that structure.
06	S:	But what if it's still true?
07	T:	That doesn't matter. In reported speech, we change the tense. That's the grammar rule. Let's keep going.

This exchange exemplifies authoritative discourse (Mortimer & Scott, 2003), where the teacher's primary aim is to transmit fixed knowledge and maintain control over the content and interaction. In doing so, the teacher exercises language power, which is defined as the ability to describe what counts as legitimate knowledge, who can speak, and how language should be used in the classroom (Cummins, 2000; Fairclough, 2013).

In Alexander's terms, this is not collective, as only the teacher addresses the learning. It is not even reciprocal, as they are students who are only listening to what the teacher is saying. It is not supportive and cumulative, as the sentence "let's keep going," in Turn 07, shows no support for students' ideas and voices. It is not purposeful since the teacher does not provide any room for discussion. The teacher, in effect, rejects or sidelines students' exploratory or critical questions (e.g., in Turn 2: "Why do we change the tense?") and reasserts rules as nonnegotiable, universal truths (e.g., in Turn 3: "Because that's the rule") and reinforces a hierarchical structure in which authority is embedded in standard linguistic norms and grammar rules. There is no space for dialogic exploration of the grammatical phenomenon or for multiple perspectives (e.g., pragmatic use of tense in reported speech when facts remain true). Student agency is limited, and uptake is evaluated strictly against correctness. The use of IRF (Initiation–Response–Feedback) sequences (Sinclair & Coulthard, 1975), with limited uptake of student input (Nassaji & Wells, 2000), exemplifies how discourse structures can regulate participation and maintain power asymmetries. While such discourse may be efficient for test preparation and rule internalization, it reflects broader sociolinguistic ideologies that equate language learning with control, conformity, and compliance. As a result, it undermines students' epistemic agency (Nystrand, 1997) and inhibits the development of critical language awareness, which is essential for recognizing how language use is linked to power, ideology, and identity (Fairclough, 2013). In the second extract, however, the dialogic discourse is evident:

Language as Power in the Language Teacher Education Ecosystem 21

01	T:	In this first session, let's talk about whether you should be allowed to use Farsi (the teacher's and students' first language [L1]) in the English classroom. What do you think?
02	S1:	I think it's helpful, especially when students are confused. It can save time.
03	T:	Interesting point. Can you give an example of when it helped you?
04	S1:	Yeah, like in high school. My teacher used Persian to explain things, and I learned easily.
05	T:	Thank you. Does anyone have a different experience?
06	S2:	I disagree. I feel like it slows down my English thinking.
07	T:	That's a valid perspective. What do others think about that?
08	S3:	Maybe it depends on the level. Beginners might need L1 more than advanced learners.
09	T:	Excellent point. I'll talk about some of my considerations, and then we'll vote.

This excerpt illustrates dialogic discourse, where knowledge is co-constructed through student voices and multiple perspectives. Crucially, the teacher reconfigures language power by decentralizing authority and distributing epistemic rights among learners (Cummins, 2000; Fairclough, 2013). Rather than using language to control or regulate participation, the teacher uses it as a resource to foster inclusion, inquiry, and negotiation. This dialogic approach aligns with what Bakhtin (1981) terms *heteroglossia*: The coexistence of multiple voices and perspectives within a single classroom dialogue, resisting monologic control over meaning.

To look at this extract from Alexander's lens, this extract reflects all five principles of dialogic teaching. The interaction is collective, as the teacher engages the whole class in a shared discussion on the role of L1 in English classrooms, inviting multiple voices into the conversation. It is reciprocal, with the teacher and students actively listening and responding to one another's ideas. For instance, the teacher encourages elaboration (Turn 03) and acknowledges differing viewpoints (Turns 06–07), allowing students to consider alternative perspectives. The talk is supportive, as students express their opinions freely without fear of judgment, and their contributions are validated with affirmations such as "interesting point" and "excellent point." The exchange is also cumulative, with S3 building on earlier points by offering a synthesized view, suggesting that L1 use may depend on learners' levels. Finally, the dialogue is purposeful, framed around a meaningful pedagogical question and concluded with a voting task (Turn 09), indicating a clear instructional goal behind the discussion. In this extract, learners are treated as legitimate knowers, with the right to question, challenge, and interpret, thus participating in the co-construction of pedagogical knowledge. The teacher's role shifts from authority figure to dialogic facilitator, promoting exploratory talk (Mercer, 2000) and fostering spaces where language becomes a medium of empowerment rather than control.

To conclude, classroom discourse can either reinforce or redistribute micro-level power relations. Authoritative discourse maintains hierarchical boundaries by privileging the teacher's voice, reducing students to passive recipients of fixed knowledge. In contrast, dialogic discourse creates space for multiple voices, critical questioning, and shared epistemic agency. When teachers adopt a dialogic stance (Alexander, 2017), classroom talk becomes a democratic process through which knowledge is negotiated rather than transmitted (Freire, 2000/1970). Such interaction supports language learning and fosters students' critical language awareness and identity formation. In short, the nature of classroom discourse goes beyond a matter of technique or style to a reflection of deeper ideological positions about power.

Within the classroom, power relations and interaction patterns play an important role. The commonly observed interactional pattern in language classrooms has long been the Initiation–Response–Evaluation (IRE) sequence (Mehan, 1979), which builds on earlier work by Sinclair and Coulthard (1975) as the Initiation–Response–Feedback (IRF) model. Both frameworks position the teacher as the initiator and evaluator of talk, reinforcing institutional authority and asymmetrical power relations. Specifically, the *I* and *F* moves (or *E* in the IRE model) belong to the teacher, while the student is limited to the *R* move. This two-to-one turn ratio systematically privileges teacher talk and decision-making, turning feedback into a power move that closes down student contributions rather than expanding them (Wells, 1993).

As an alternative to this asymmetric structure, LTE programs now advocate strategies for mitigating the authoritative tendencies embedded in IRF. For instance, prolonging the *R* turn allows learners to elaborate on their responses and take ownership of the learning process. Similarly, replacing *Evaluation* with *Feedback* (in IRF) is intended to foster dialogic interaction and openness. Nonetheless, the fundamental power imbalance persists due to the unequal turn-taking distribution. To address this, Tajeddin and Kamali (2020) proposed extending the sequence to Initiation–Response–Feedback–Uptake (IRFU) to allow learners a follow-up move (*Uptake*) in order to reframe or expand their contributions. This shift holds promise for redistributing discourse control more equitably between teachers and students, thus contributing to a more dialogic and democratic pedagogy. However, this model has yet to gain widespread recognition or empirical testing in LTE.

More radically, some scholars suggest that even the *I* move, traditionally associated with teacher control, can be relinquished to learners. Dogme ELT (Meddings & Thornbury, 2009) emphasizes emergent language and learner-initiated discourse. In such classrooms, students are encouraged to initiate topics, ask questions, and guide the flow of interaction. This move toward learner-centeredness challenges the monologic tendencies of traditional classroom talk and repositions students as active meaning-makers. Yet, even in Dogme-inspired environments, the teacher retains institutional authority and gatekeeping roles and decides which student contributions to legitimize, how long to explore them, and when to move on. The teacher's control over topic development, turn allocation, and repair sequences continues to reproduce power hierarchies in subtle ways, even in ostensibly dialogic settings (Nassaji & Wells, 2000).

To further the discussion on classroom interaction, I consider teachers' questioning. The questioning strategies teachers use further reinforce or disrupt power dynamics (Hudson & Pletcher, 2020). Display questions (those with known answers) tend to position the teacher as the knower and the student as the responder, reinforcing traditional authority (Aguiar et al., 2010). These questions typically serve to assess students' knowledge rather than promote genuine engagement or co-construction of meaning. In contrast, referential questions (genuine inquiries) invite more extended student turns and are associated with more egalitarian discourse patterns, as they position learners as contributors of knowledge rather than passive recipients (Tajeddin & Kamali, 2023). When learners are asked authentic questions, they are more likely to engage in reflective and critical thinking, which can foster deeper learning.

Similarly, feedback practices can either shut down dialogue (e.g., when limited to brief evaluative comments such as "good" or "correct") or open it up through scaffolding, clarification requests, and prompting further elaboration (Mercer, 2000). Feedback that encourages elaboration supports dialogic teaching by creating opportunities for negotiation of meaning and collaborative knowledge construction, which shifts classroom power relations toward a more shared and participatory model (Kamali et al., 2025). Certain feedback techniques have been identified as supportive of promoting power equilibrium in the classroom. For instance, elicitation ('asking learners some questions to elicit the correct form'; Tajeddin & Kamali, 2020, p. 334), a strategy used in teacher feedback that encourages student voice and agency, has been shown to be effective (Nassaji, 2007).

All in all, instruction, questioning, and feedback are not neutral pedagogical tools but are deeply implicated in the enactment of power. Teachers' discursive choices can either sustain hierarchical classroom structures or support more participatory, student-centered interactions. Thus, understanding these elements as power moves opens space for a critical pedagogy (Freire, 2000/1970) that foregrounds voice, agency, and social justice in language education and LTE. The challenge remains: How to move beyond superficial modifications to classroom talk and embrace deeper structural shifts in pedagogy.

2.3 Micro-Resistance

Before I begin this section, I would like to define resistance, which, like many other concepts, can have various definitions. In the words of Sorensen (2008), "Resistance is a response to power that challenges oppression and domination" (p. 170). Micro-resistance in language classrooms, then, refers to subtle, everyday acts of teachers and students used to challenge, negotiate, or subvert dominant power structures without direct confrontation. For the purpose of this Element, I will focus on three main acts of micro-resistance: silence, humor, and translanguaging.

A significant, yet often overlooked, factor in practicing or resisting LaP in the classroom is silence. Paradoxically, silence can function as a discursive tool through which power and hegemony are enacted. It should be borne in mind that silence has different meanings in different cultures. For example, Harumi (2011) found that one of the reasons for the silence of the students in the Japanese EFL classroom is Confucian ethics, which appreciate silence. My experience of working with teachers with different nationalities from different cultures in LTE programs confirms this view. Once, one of my Korean trainees complained about why her classmates talked so much in class. She asked, "Don't they think they are taking the time that belongs to everyone?" while their classmates thought that this was a way of showing themselves active in class.

Silence is traditionally associated "with powerlessness, particularly in relationships characterized by power imbalances" (McLaren, 2016, p. 3). However, "while power inflicts silence, silence also has the capacity to destabilize existing powers and structures of control" (McLaren, 2016, p. 3). "Silence appears as a rich communicative resource whose understanding requires the sophistication of a fine-grained, interdisciplinary analysis" (Jaworski & Sachdev, 1998, p. 273). For example, sometimes, instead of shouting, teachers decide to remain silent to attract attention (Gilmore, 1985).

Building on this, Bao (2023) argues that the value or problem of silence is not inherent but depends on who is judging it and on local responsiveness norms; even short response delays can be misread as silence, so evaluation must remain context-sensitive. Pedagogically, talk and silence should be coordinated: forcing speech when learners need quiet (or imposing quiet when they are ready to speak) can hinder development, and listening-and-thinking ("vicarious participation"; Northedge, 2003, p. 30) should be recognized as learning in its own right. Bao further urges teachers to regulate the timing and amount of their own verbalization, protecting reflective spaces instead of filling every gap, and to make explicit when silence is for thinking and when speech is expected.

"Cultural attitudes" (and, in my view, generic awareness) "to discourse [of] silence ... [is] very important in assessing the perceived success of speakers in getting their point across" (Jaworski, 1992, p. 6). Silence can sometimes be mobilized as a resource of power; however, the link between longer pauses and greater dominance is culture-bound rather than universal. In some rhetorical traditions (e.g., Western political oratory), strategic pauses can project control and authority, whereas in many Asian contexts, silence may index attentiveness, respect, or facework rather than dominance (Bao, 2023). Accordingly, interpretations of silence should be grounded in local participation norms and cultural expectations. This phenomenon is equally relevant in educational settings, where silence can have various functions in teachers' classroom practices (Forrest, 2013). In the classroom, silence can act as a tool in teachers' hands for different purposes, such as "(1) preparing the classroom for learning; (2) teaching, questioning, and facilitating learning; (3) reflecting and thinking; and (4) behavioural management" (Tan et al., 2025, p. 331). However, it can act oppositely when it is used when the teacher is not confident enough to talk in the class, for example, when an observer observes a class. For students, on the other hand, silence can act as a critical tool to resist power imbalance in the classroom (Cervantes-Soon, 2025). Sedova and Navratilova (2020), in a study on students' silence, highlighted that silence in the classroom can reflect students' strategic positioning. High-achieving students use silence to assert competence and gain trust, while lower-achieving students use it to avoid exposure and maintain a low profile. Thus, silence operates as both agency and self-protection within classroom power dynamics.

Another aspect of practicing and resisting power in any microsystem, including language classrooms, is humor. It is a difficult term to define, as "what one person views as funny might not be shared by others" (Humonen & Whittle, 2025, p. 347). This phenomenon "stands at the intersection of politics, culture, and society" (Beck & Spencer, 2025, p. 3); therefore, it can be analyzed within various disciplines. In the LTE microsystem, humor can function as a way of humiliating less-powerful individuals, often referred to as its dark side (Plester, 2016). Humor can act as a subtle tool of control (Butler, 2013), supporting discriminatory behaviors and fostering exclusion within professional settings

(Watts, 2007), such as language classrooms. Rather than building solidarity, it may reinforce social hierarchies and increase the emotional or professional distance between individuals (Holmes & Marra, 2002).

Humor is also a subtle yet effective tool for challenging dominant classroom norms, negotiating power dynamics, and expressing agency. In language learning settings, students and teachers alike may use humor to resist rigid pedagogical expectations, critique materials, or push back against the authority of the curriculum. Humor can help maintain solidarity while simultaneously challenging power relations, making it a socially acceptable means of voicing discontent or disagreement (Holmes, 2006). Billig (2005) also emphasizes that humor is inherently ideological, capable of revealing underlying tensions within interpersonal interactions. In this way, humorous remarks, sarcasm, or playful language use in the classroom can signal nonviolent resistance (Sorensen, 2008) without causing direct conflict, allowing participants to reframe power relations and co-construct more inclusive learning spaces.

Last but not least, the concept of translanguaging comes into play. Although this nomenclature is new (Baker, 2001), the concept has been with us for a long time with different names, such as code-switching, L1 use, to name a few (with some differences; García, 2009). Prior to these developments, seeing as taboo in language classrooms, the use of L1 has long been prohibited in the classroom, and the teachers who permitted this approach were criticized for allegedly undermining or compromising the students' educational progress (Martin, 2005).

Since its advent, translanguaging has faced three major critiques (Turner & Lin, 2024): First, its deconstructivist stance challenges the existence of distinct languages as cognitive entities, potentially weakening efforts to protect language rights and support multilingual education. Second, critics argue that despite its promise, translanguaging lacks genuine transformative power, as it does little to address structural inequalities or achieve socio-economic change. Third, the term is seen as overly broad, conflating descriptive, theoretical, and ideological functions, and overlapping with long-established concepts like code-switching, which can lead to conceptual ambiguity.

Despite ongoing critiques, translanguaging contributes meaningfully to fostering equity and shifting power dynamics in language classrooms because of "the central focus ... on the disruption of linguistic hierarchies and addressing social inequity" (Turner & Lin, 2024, p. 2). By encouraging learners to use their entire linguistic repertoires, it challenges the dominance of standardized language forms and affirms the identities of students from diverse backgrounds (Yilmaz, 2021). This approach repositions classroom norms away from monolingual expectations and toward inclusive practices that recognize and value all languages (Wei & Lin, 2019). Although it may fall short of fully addressing systemic inequalities on its own, translanguaging creates opportunities for more balanced participation, greater linguistic confidence, and the meaningful inclusion of minoritized languages and cultures in educational contexts.

In summary, this section has highlighted how micro-resistance in language classrooms takes diverse forms, including silence, humor, and translanguaging, that both challenge and negotiate power dynamics in subtle yet impactful ways. Silence can serve as a strategic tool for both asserting authority and resisting marginalization, shaped deeply by cultural norms. Humor operates ambivalently, sometimes reinforcing hierarchies but also enabling nonconfrontational resistance and solidarity. Translanguaging, despite facing critiques regarding its conceptual scope and transformative power, offers a powerful means to disrupt linguistic hierarchies and promote equity by validating learners' full linguistic repertoires. Together, these acts reveal the complex ways teachers and students engage with power in the classroom. In the next section, we will discuss how these issues can be addressed within the LTE programs to better support equitable and empowering language teaching practices.

2.4 Addressing Microsystem Issues of LaP in LTE Programs

The very first thing to do to address issues of power and resistance in LTE programs is to raise teachers' awareness regarding this issue and explicitly train them to recognize how power operates at the classroom level. As Freedman (2007) and Ellsworth (1989) suggest, teachers who become aware of their own power are better positioned to negotiate and employ it ethically and reflectively in the classroom. This self-awareness forms the foundation for fostering equitable and empowering learning spaces. LTE programs must, therefore, go beyond technical skill-building and offer pedagogical tools that support critical reflection, inclusive communication practices, and resistance to oppressive classroom dynamics.

A crucial starting point is supporting the development of LTI and agency. As numerous studies highlight (e.g., Barkhuizen, 2017; Tajeddin & Yazan, 2024), LTI emerges dynamically through social, emotional, and linguistic experiences. When LTE programs make space for teachers to explore their sociocultural backgrounds, positionalities, and evolving beliefs, they foster a sense of agency: Teachers' capacity to make principled pedagogical choices in response to contextual realities (Priestley et al., 2015). Recognizing this, LTE may include dialogic autobiographical activities or narrative inquiry projects to help teachers reflect on how their identities intersect with power and pedagogical practice (De Costa, 2025).

Genuine questioning is another key component. Teacher talk often mirrors hierarchical dynamics, where questions are used to test rather than to invite exploration (Walsh, 2011). Training teachers to ask open-ended, dialogic, and curiosity-driven questions not only fosters student engagement but also redistributes authority in classroom discourse (Boyd & Markarian, 2011). Drawing on the concept of loop input in LTE (see Woodward, 2003), such programs should model dialogic teaching by incorporating dialogic strategies into their training sessions and embedding dialogic feedback cycles within practicum components.

Alongside this, peer feedback can serve as a democratic and dialogic tool (Hornstein et al., 2025). Traditional top-down feedback structures can reinforce power imbalances and limit teachers' voices in their own development. Instead, LTE programs should promote collaborative peer feedback grounded in trust, mutual respect, and critical engagement (Carless & Boud, 2018). By learning how to promote giving and receiving feedback among students, teachers can develop reflexivity and a sense of professional community.

Translanguaging must also be reframed as a central principle of LTE, more than a classroom practice. It offers a framework for resisting linguistic hierarchies and affirming the full linguistic and cultural repertoires of teachers and learners (Beiler & Villacañas de Castro, 2025). LTE programs should critically examine language ideologies, support candidates' reflections on their own language practices, and design micro-teaching and materials development tasks that legitimize multilingualism in practice (Yilmaz, 2021). In doing so, teacher-learners cultivate pedagogical agency and challenge deficit views of bi/multilingualism.

Finally, reflective practice binds these threads together. Reflection in LTE should encourage techniques that can help teachers practice their voice in the LTE ecosystem and give voice and power to students (Farrell & Farrell, 2025). Through structured journaling, dialogues, and collaborative reflection (Chan & Aubrey, 2024; Kamali & Javahery, 2025), teachers can explore how silence, humor, identity, and resistance shape their teaching. These activities can serve as safe spaces where emerging teachers grapple with dilemmas and develop an ethical stance towards language power and pedagogy.

In sum, LTE microsystems can address the tensions of power and resistance by supporting LTI formation, fostering agency, and embedding transformative pedagogies such as genuine questioning, peer feedback, translanguaging, and critical reflection.

3 LaP in LTE Mesosystem

Language Teaching Organizations (LTOs) are institutions that design, deliver, and assure the quality of language education programs (such as private language schools, university language centers, and K–12 departments) by overseeing curriculum, assessment, teacher recruitment and development, learner support, and compliance with accreditation and regulatory standards. They are treated here as a mesosystem because they sit at the junction where multiple microsystems (teachers, teacher educators, classrooms, students, mentoring, and their parents) intersect with macrosystem forces (state policy, accreditation regimes, corporate testing and publishing, global language markets). In Bronfenbrenner's ecological terms, the mesosystem is the layer that organizes relations among microsystems; it mediates, translates, and sometimes transforms wider ideological currents into the routines of everyday work (Bronfenbrenner, 1979, 1993). LTOs perform precisely this mediating function: They convert policy into handbooks, standards into observation rubrics, market pressures into syllabi, and institutional ideologies into best practice scripts. Because this translation work is predominantly linguistic (policies, emails, meetings, feedback forms, PD workshops), LTOs are a privileged site for examining how language operates as power. Put differently, LTOs are a field in which specific linguistic capitals are authorized and circulated (Bourdieu, 1991), and where hegemony is maintained or unsettled through discourse (Fairclough, 2013). Analyzing the LTO as a mesosystem, therefore, allows us to trace how macro-level ideologies (which will be discussed in the next section) are reproduced, negotiated, or resisted in the meso-level discursive practices that govern teachers' professional lives.

3.1 Discursive Practices in LTOs

Any LTO is a unique society with its own culture, norms, standards, and power dynamics. In LTOs, discursive practices, that is, structured ways of using language that carry ideological and institutional significance (Fairclough, 2013), are more than routine ways of using language and are mechanisms through which institutional power is exercised, normalized, and sometimes contested. Drawing on a sociocultural understanding of discourse (Fairclough, 2013), such practices include both formal communication (e.g., policy documents, staff handbooks, official memos) and informal interactions (e.g., teacher-room conversations, email tone, meeting discourse) (Thornborrow, 2014). These practices shape how roles, responsibilities, and identities are constructed within the organization (Macaulay, 2025). From a mesosystemic perspective (Bronfenbrenner, 1979), these discourses reflect the interface between individual actors (e.g., teachers) and the institutional structures that govern their practice, often reproducing hegemonic norms under the guise of PD or organizational growth (Rubin & Tily, 2021).

One key site where discursive power manifests is in institutional policy language. Policies in LTOs (especially those regarding teacher conduct, assessment practices, or curriculum design) are often framed through seemingly neutral, bureaucratic language but in fact it produces "policy coloniality as a political rationality that (re)produces racialized realities, dualizing populations into those deserving of policy attention and those perceived as dangerous and in need of control" (Jhagroe & Salazar-Morales, 2025, p. 1). Terms such as "best practice," "learner-centeredness," or "professional behavior" which are imposed by those in power and should be followed by less powerful individuals are rarely defined but widely invoked. This ambiguity serves an ideological function: It allows managers to invoke policy selectively, often to discipline or guide behavior in ways that align with broader institutional goals (McLaughlin et al., 2025).

For instance, "best practice," which was attacked by Prabhu in 1990 with a seminal paper titled *There is no best method – Why?* and continues to be attacked by different scholars, prominently Kumaravadivelu (1994), is articulated in most LTOs, where their way of teaching is considered the norm, which is the most efficient and useful (Canagarajah, 2018). Such language limits teacher autonomy and makes institutional mandates appear objective and apolitical. In many cases, it also reinforces dominant ideologies and power relations, privileging methods associated with certain linguistic or cultural norms (often those of the Global North) while marginalizing localized or experiential knowledge and positioning some teachers in what Fallas-Escobar and Pentón Herrera (2022) describe as *raciolinguistic struggles*: Navigating how their language practices are racialized and policed within institutional contexts. As a result, teachers may feel compelled to adopt prescriptive practices that do not align with their students' needs or their own professional judgment. This ongoing tension between institutional norms and pedagogical diversity highlights the need to re-evaluate what counts as *best* and to shift toward more pluralistic, context-responsive understandings of effective teaching.

Moreover, the pervasiveness of audit culture (Shore & Wright, 2015) within LTOs has intensified the bureaucratization of discourses, where terms like "performance indicators" and "quality assurance" are normalized and often prioritized over meaningful pedagogical dialogue. This shift reflects a growing emphasis on managerialism and performativity (Fitzgerald & Hall, 2021), where teaching is increasingly framed through measurable outputs rather than contextual understanding or reflective practice (Neophytou, 2025). As a result, teachers may feel pressured to conform to standardized practices and external benchmarks, often at the expense of creativity, autonomy, and responsiveness to learner needs (Kamali, 2014). Over time, such an environment fosters a culture of compliance, discouraging innovation and marginalizing alternative pedagogical approaches that cannot be easily quantified or audited. The dominance of audit logic also risks silencing critical conversations around equity, identity, and professional growth, as these concerns rarely fit within audit frameworks (Jary, 2013). Consequently, educational quality becomes equated with surface-level accountability rather than deeper engagement with learning processes, and teachers are positioned as service providers rather than professionals with situated expertise and judgment (Ball, 2003).

Overall, examining discursive practices in LTOs reveals how language functions as a key mediator of institutional power, ideology, and resistance. The mesosystem becomes a crucial level of analysis, foregrounding how macro-level ideologies (e.g., neoliberalism, managerialism) are enacted and challenged in the micro-interactions and discursive routines of institutional life.

3.2 Professional Development

In this section, I use PD to refer specifically to training sessions and workshops rather than broader activities such as mentoring. PD in language teaching institutions is often framed as an unquestionable good, a cornerstone of quality assurance and teacher growth. In practice, however, institutional PD is rarely a neutral process. The structure, content, and delivery of in-service training and workshops are deeply shaped by institutional agendas, quality frameworks, and accreditation requirements, all of which embed certain ideological positions about language. These positions, while rarely made explicit, often reproduce hegemonic norms by promoting narrow definitions of linguistic "correctness," privileging particular standardized varieties, and reinforcing long-standing associations between language authority and nativeness (Bouchard, 2020; Holliday, 2022).

In my own experience, I ran a workshop at my workplace in which I invited teachers to write down the problems students most frequently brought to tutorial sessions and then to describe how they typically addressed them. The outcomes were compiled into a document, creating a shared reference of possible solutions that teachers could consult in the future. On the surface, this appeared to be a genuinely teacher-led initiative (Macias, 2017) that valued practitioner knowledge. However, even this format revealed the underlying power imbalance, particularly the linguistic or discursive one. The way problems were articulated and the language used to frame solutions were subtly shaped by institutional discourse, which privileges terms such as *learner autonomy* or *target language use* framed in standardized, monolingual ways. These linguistic preferences are closely tied to the institution's operational definitions of quality and professionalism, themselves linked to performance indicators, observation rubrics, and curriculum standards. As a result, contributions that adopted the institution's preferred linguistic framing were more likely to be taken up, while those expressed through alternative or locally grounded discourses tended to remain peripheral. This mirrors Freeman and Johnson's (1998) observation that teacher learning is socially situated yet bounded by institutional structures that determine what counts as valid professional knowledge.

Institutional PD agendas frequently draw on prescriptive linguistic standards, imported curricula, and accreditation-linked performance criteria. In English language education, the Common European Framework of Reference (CEFR), International English Language Testing System (IELTS) band descriptors, and British or American English style norms are widely adopted for convenience, prestige, and perceived international credibility. Similar patterns are evident in other languages: In French, Parisian pronunciation and usage often serve as the institutional benchmark, marginalizing francophone African or Canadian varieties; in Spanish, Castilian norms from Spain are privileged over Latin American forms in pronunciation workshops and writing standards; in Arabic, Modern Standard Arabic is upheld as the sole formal variety, sidelining widely used regional dialects in pedagogical materials; and in Mandarin Chinese, Putonghua norms dominate, with local dialects and topolects treated as deviations from the standard. While these tools and norms can bring consistency and comparability, they also establish a hierarchy of linguistic forms, presenting certain varieties as inherently more legitimate. This has been critiqued in multiple contexts for marginalizing locally grounded pedagogies and sidelining community language practices (Blommaert, 2010; Canagarajah, 2018).

Even when workshops are framed as practical skill-building, they often prioritize surface-level competencies that can be observed and measured, such as applying a uniform error correction technique, replicating a model lesson sequence, or adhering to prescriptive pronunciation targets. While such training satisfies quality assurance protocols, it aligns with "instrumental professionalism" (Bakker & Ter Avest, 2019, p. 2), where teacher development is evaluated by compliance with externally defined benchmarks rather than by the capacity to adapt, innovate, or respond to local linguistic ecologies. The emphasis on measurable outputs can inadvertently discourage exploratory practice (Allwright, 2005), favoring performance conformity over professional judgment.

Woodward's (2003) concept of loop input offers a useful contrast here. Loop input designs PD so that the mode of training mirrors the pedagogical approach it seeks to promote, encouraging teachers to experience, adapt, and critically reflect on practices in real time. In the context of language-focused PD, this might mean modeling translanguaging in the training itself or inviting participants to redesign materials to reflect local varieties. Yet, in many institutions, the flexibility required for loop input is at odds with the need for standardization in observation checklists and accreditation audits (Mockler, 2020). As a result, even conscientious trainers may feel compelled to prioritize institutionally approved models over adaptive, locally relevant practices.

The persistence of native-speakerism in institutional PD remains one of the clearest indicators of how hegemonic language norms are reproduced. In Spanish language programs, Castilian norms often dominate PD content (del Valle, 2014); in French, Parisian varieties are elevated (Lodge, 2004); and in Arabic, Modern Standard Arabic is prioritized over local dialects (Towler, 2025). Phillipson's (1992) critique of linguistic imperialism remains relevant here, as does Holliday's (2006) account of how native-speaker norms are naturalized in professional discourse. In institutional PD, these norms may be embedded in model lesson videos, pronunciation workshops, or assessment exemplars, shaping teachers' perceptions of what constitutes "target-like" performance. Even initiatives that claim to embrace plurilingualism may do so superficially, adding token examples without allowing them to reshape core assessment or observation standards (Marlina & Giri, 2014).

Institutional gatekeeping is also evident in how teacher voices are included, or excluded, in PD planning. While teacher-led initiatives are increasingly common, the themes, materials, and follow-up actions often remain under administrative control. Research by Borg (2015) on teacher cognition highlights that teachers' professional beliefs and experiential knowledge are often underutilized in institutional decision-making. In my workshop, for example, contributions that aligned with the institution's prescribed language policies were taken forward, while suggestions that introduced local language practices or more flexible use of multilingual repertoires were absent from formal implementation. This selective uptake reinforces a feedback loop: Teachers are encouraged to speak, but only within parameters set by institutional ideology. Dominant institutional systems, therefore, determine whose voices are legitimized (Dovchin & Marlina, 2025) and whose are marginalized, particularly through raciolinguistic processes that intertwine language legitimacy with racialized identity (Fallas-Escobar & Pentón Herrera, 2022).

Another driver of norm reproduction is the direct link between PD outcomes and performance evaluation. Many institutions use PD as preparatory training for meeting observation criteria, student feedback expectations, and accreditation requirements, along with teachers' development. This convergence means that teachers are incentivized to internalize institutional definitions of effective language use because these definitions directly impact career progression, contract renewal, and professional reputation. PD in such contexts serves a dual function: skill enhancement and institutional socialization (Pennington & Richards, 2016). The latter, while not inherently negative, can lead to a narrowing of pedagogical diversity when socialization is tightly bound to a single linguistic model.

Reimagining PD within these constraints requires acknowledging its ideological role in the LTE mesosystem. While PD will inevitably reflect institutional goals, greater transparency about the linguistic ideologies embedded in training content could open space for negotiated adaptation. Institutional calendars could include teacher-designed modules with minimal administrative interference, allowing for local innovation without discarding standardization entirely (Dodman, 2021). Embedding reflective dialogue, perhaps under the guise of "collaborative reflection" sessions, could also permit critical discussion of norms without triggering resistance from policy-makers (Kamali & Javahery, 2025).

By recognizing PD as a site where institutional priorities and language ideologies intersect, teacher educators and administrators can move toward a model that supports both coherence and contextual responsiveness. Without this awareness, PD risks continuing as a mechanism for the reproduction of hegemonic language norms, shaping teachers in what they believe counts as legitimate language in the classroom.

3.3 Observation Feedback

Observation in LTOs serves four main purposes (Malderez, 2003): training, development, assessment, and research. In practice, however, these events are rarely neutral; they are sites where language, authority, and professional norms intersect (O'Leary, 2013). For many teachers, being observed is about presenting their pedagogical skills while simultaneously responding to the subtle power relations embedded in the process. The observation feedback "happens after a lesson has been taught and observed" (Copland & Donaghue, 2019, p. 402). It is the planned, post-lesson dialogue in which an observer and the observed teacher draw on specific lesson evidence to interpret practice against agreed criteria, affirm strengths, identify development needs, and co-construct actionable next steps (Bailey, 2006; O'Leary, 2020). The way feedback is framed, worded, and delivered can either empower teachers or reinforce institutional hierarchies. Advanced teacher training courses, such as Cambridge DELTA (Diploma in Teaching English to Speakers of Other Languages) or Trinity DipTESOL (Diploma in Teaching English to Speakers of Other Languages), position observation and feedback as central components of professional formation, beyond fulfilling procedural requirements. For example, Unit 2 of Trinity DipTESOL tasks candidates with creating context-specific observation tools, which encourage them to consider both what is observed and how post-observation discourse unfolds. Similarly, the Cambridge Train the Trainer course (discontinued from 2023) devoted an entire module to the discourse of observation feedback. Within this framework, four key types of feedback are typically discussed: directive, alternative, collaborative, and non-directive. Each of these reveals different configurations of teacher autonomy and observer authority, and illustrates how professional regulation is enacted through talk.

Directive feedback enacts a hierarchical model of PD in which language serves as a mechanism of authority and control. The observer's evaluative language positions them as the expert, often reproducing institutional power dynamics and reinforcing normative standards of *good teaching* (Copland, 2012). This top-down approach can marginalize teachers' voices, as decisions about effective pedagogy (Kamali, 2024) are linguistically framed by the observer, not negotiated. As such, directive feedback reflects what Foucault (1979) terms "disciplinary power," where control is exercised not through coercion but through discourse that shapes professional identity and behavior.

Alternative feedback reflects a partial shift in the power dynamic, introducing space for teacher agency while still maintaining a level of observer authority. The language used often combines suggestion with inquiry, allowing teachers to engage but within boundaries shaped by the observer's interpretations of the lesson (Copland & Neokleous, 2011). While this model reduces overt asymmetry, it may still operate within "soft regulation" (Garsten & Jacobsson, 2013, p. 2), where power is exercised through the subtle framing of pedagogical possibilities rather than open co-construction.

Collaborative feedback embodies a more dialogic and egalitarian use of language, with power distributed more evenly between observer and teacher. In this model, interaction is characterized by mutual questioning, reflective dialogue, and shared meaning-making (Mann & Walsh, 2017). Language becomes a tool for co-construction rather than correction, supporting what Hunt (2018) describes as dialogic professional learning. The collaborative approach aligns with sociocultural perspectives that view learning and development as mediated through interaction and negotiation rather than imposed evaluation.

Nondirective feedback represents the most teacher-centered model, where the observer's linguistic role is primarily facilitative rather than evaluative. Here, power is decentralized; the teacher's voice dominates, and the observer listens, paraphrases, and prompts reflection. This echoes dialogic models of teacher development (Boyd & Markarian, 2011), in which the teacher constructs meaning through guided self-discovery. The use of open-ended questions and withholding of judgment fosters autonomy and professional agency, resisting dominant discourses of surveillance and managerialism often found in teacher evaluation systems (Pennycook, 2021).

While the four models, that is, directive, alternative, collaborative, and nondirective, represent different approaches to feedback following an observation, they still operate within a structure where observation is externally initiated and often led by an appointed observer. In contrast, *Narrative Self-Observation (NSO)*, which Jason Anderson and I recently developed (Kamali & Anderson, 2025), reimagines observation itself as a teacher-led process. Here, the teacher decides the focus, conducts the observation by narrating and analyzing their own experience, and invites a *collaborator* (not an evaluator) into a reflective dialogue. This shift in both process and power dynamic makes NSO deeply bottom-up and agentive. Rather than being observed, the teacher becomes a co-researcher of their own practice, and any "feedback" emerges from mutual sense-making. NSO thus transcends traditional observation-feedback binaries by embedding professional learning within teacher narrative, identity, and inquiry.

To ground these theoretical perspectives in lived experience, the next section presents a case study based on a reflective interview between me and a fellow teacher educator. In this dialogue, we reflect on our experiences with different observation feedback models as teachers and teacher educators and critically examine how issues of power, language, and professional regulation emerged in our observation and feedback practices.

3.3.1 A Case Study

Parsa (a pseudonym) is a professional teacher educator and an educational supervisor at an Iranian language institute. He is a PhD candidate in ELT and holds the Trinity CertTESOL (Certificate in Teaching English to Speakers of Other Languages) and Cambridge Train the Trainer certifications. With over seven years of experience, he designs and delivers general English as a Foreign Language (EFL) teacher training courses as well as PD workshops for both preservice and in-service teachers. His responsibilities also include syllabus and curriculum design for various EFL programs tailored to diverse learner needs.

Language as Power in the Language Teacher Education Ecosystem 37

Actively engaged in research on teacher training, he integrates current academic insights into practical training to help teachers develop key classroom skills and overcome challenges. He fully consented to participating in this research and sharing his professional experiences, with the understanding that all identifying details would remain confidential in accordance with ethical research guidelines.

Parsa's role spans both preservice and in-service contexts. In preservice settings, he is involved in reviewing lesson plans before the observed lesson and delivering formal feedback afterward. In in-service contexts, the observation tends to be shorter (20 minutes of observation followed by a 15-minute reflection) but still includes a structured feedback session. Despite the differences in audience, the institutional goals remain similar: *outcomes matter*. According to him, school managers expect feedback to focus on tangible skills like productive language use and require specific classroom discourse features – such as concept-checking questions (CCQs) – to be present. Additionally, external stakeholders, particularly parents, exert implicit pressure to demonstrate learner success and visible classroom engagement. Parsa interestingly mentioned the interconnection of different layers of the LTE ecosystem by discussing microsystem (family) and mesosystem (institution):

> For example, sometimes students' parents ask other people to assist them in assessing their children, and parents expect the Institute to work on the productive skills of their children, and the manager expects me to train teachers who can work on the productive skills. So, it's a kind of circle. It's a circle of action.

The structure of feedback sessions in his context fluctuates between directive and collaborative models. He noted that although he prefers to engage teachers through questioning and reflective prompts, institutional hierarchies often shape how much room there is for dialogic interaction. "As a teacher, my observers were always in control. Supervisors were in power," he recalled. This highlights a long-standing tradition of top-down observation practices. While he sometimes takes a directive approach, especially with dominant teachers, he emphasized the importance of adapting tone and approach based on experience and individual differences (Javahery & Kamali, 2023; Kamali & Javahery, 2024). When it comes to novice teachers, he exercises greater care and is aware that his language plays a formative role in shaping their emerging professional identities.

Parsa acknowledged institutional expectations to adopt a dominant stance during feedback, even recounting a moment:

> I never forget this quote from one of the managers that I used to work for, she said 'Feel free to fire anyone you want when you want. If they don't listen to

you, fire them' ... I didn't want to take advantage of this freedom, you know ... because I knew that I could be the victim.

Such comments (i.e., Feel free to fire anyone you want) exemplify the broader system of power that underpins observation, where teacher educators are not just assessors but enforcers of institutional norms. He shared how this authority is often exercised linguistically through tone, mitigation strategies, and explicit directives that indirectly regulate how teachers speak, question, and interact in the classroom. Mitigation, in particular, was highlighted as a key linguistic strategy: While feedback must point out areas for improvement, the language must be calibrated to preserve rapport and reduce face-threatening acts (Brown & Levinson, 1978).

The case study also underscores how institutional discourse can enforce specific methodological preferences. For example, Parsa described being pressured by a manager who strongly favored the Total Physical Response (TPR) method (Asher, 1969) in language teaching, despite his own reservations about its effectiveness across all contexts. He recalled situations in which he had to endorse certain practices during feedback, not because they aligned with his pedagogical beliefs, but because institutional expectations demanded it. This reveals how feedback can serve to normalize certain teaching ideologies under the guise of "professional standards," sidelining teacher agency and contextual variation. Although he was particularly aware of how his linguistic choices during feedback could either reproduce or resist institutional discourse, he acknowledged the pressure to "produce yes-men." He, in turn, viewed collaborative feedback as a way of modeling professional dialogue as a means of resisting top-down managerialism.

In discussing the empowering or regulatory nature of feedback, he mentioned tone and word choice, noting that authority is not just in what is said but in *how* it is said. According to him, empowering feedback allows space for the teacher's voice to emerge, particularly through greater teacher talking time and the opportunity to express concerns or reflect on their own practices. "It's about how much the teacher can talk about her own concerns," he noted, while stressing the importance of equitable dialogue in feedback sessions.

Finally, Parsa emphasized that observation feedback cannot be fully understood without considering the broader sociocultural context. Factors such as institutional culture, individual differences, emotional intelligence, and even the connotations of praise all influence how feedback is delivered and received. "It's complicated," he concluded, pointing out that feedback is pedagogical, political, emotional, and situated.

This reflective dialogue between me and Parsa illustrates the intricate interplay between language, power, and professionalism in observation feedback. Even well-intentioned teacher educators must navigate institutional demands, cultural expectations, and interpersonal dynamics that can subtly or overtly shape the feedback discourse (Heron et al., 2023). While collaborative and reflective practices offer a partial resistance to top-down control, more transformative approaches (see Kamali and Anderson [2025] on NSO) may be needed to fully reposition teachers as agents in their own PD. As Parsa's experience shows, the politics of observation are embedded in the smallest linguistic choices, yet their consequences ripple outward into the shaping of teacher identities and institutional cultures.

3.4 Addressing Mesosystem Issues of LaP in LTOs

The first step toward addressing LaP issues in LTOs is *recognition*. Without acknowledging that institutional discourse, policy language, and feedback practices can reproduce inequity, no meaningful change can occur. Noel Burch's conscious incompetence stage in the Four Stages of Competence provides a useful entry point (Broadwell, 1969): Both managers and teachers must move from being unaware of problematic practices (*unconscious incompetence*) to consciously recognizing and admitting them (*conscious incompetence*). For example, awareness that *best practice* rhetoric may marginalize local pedagogies creates space for questioning and reimagining these standards. Such consciousness-raising should be embedded into institutional training cycles, ensuring that all stakeholders (teachers, teacher trainers, and managers) can critically examine the linguistic and ideological underpinnings of their work.

A second consideration is avoiding misaligned promotions that inadvertently entrench problematic practices. The Peter Principle (Peter & Hull, 1969) warns against promoting individuals solely because they excel in their current role, such as an excellent classroom teacher being moved into teacher training, without ensuring they have the skills, critical awareness, and dispositions required for their new responsibilities. In LTOs, this can lead to teacher trainers or managers reproducing the same hegemonic discourses they once resisted (McMain, 2023; Pennycook, 2021), simply because they have not been prepared to explore the politics of language and power at the mesosystem level. Structured pathways, such as the International Diploma in Language Teaching Management (IDLTM), can prepare future leaders to critically engage with institutional discourse, handle power responsibly, and avoid perpetuating top-down managerialism.

Teacher-led PD is a powerful counterbalance to centrally dictated agendas. When teachers themselves identify priorities, design content, and lead sessions, they both gain professional agency and challenge the default alignment of PD with managerial objectives. Teacher-led PD could take the form of Professional Learning Communities (PLCs) (Ongoing, collaborative groups of educators who engage in collective inquiry and evidence-informed action to improve teaching and student learning, sharing responsibility for outcomes through structured dialogue, reflection, and iterative cycles of improvement; Stoll et al., 2006), inquiry groups, or local research projects, with institutional support provided for resources, time, and dissemination (Holden, 2002; Stoll et al., 2017). Such models value experiential knowledge, foregrounding classroom realities over imported templates. Because institutional hierarchies tend to reassert themselves, implementing genuinely teacher-led discourse requires deliberate safeguards that allow teachers to speak openly without judgment or evaluation.

Collaborative reflection is another key practice. Unlike standard observation-feedback structures, collaborative reflection sessions focus on mutual sense-making between peers or between teachers and managers (Kamali & Javahery, 2025). This allows for a rebalancing of power. Rather than being the passive recipients of "corrections," teachers actively co-construct understandings of practice. Embedding collaborative reflection into observation cycles, whether through peer observation, post-lesson dialogues, or teacher narratives, helps resist the surveillance function of evaluation and instead turns it into a space for professional growth (Mann & Walsh, 2017).

Giving teachers a sustained voice in decision-making is crucial (Good, 2018). Token consultation can reinforce, rather than challenge, existing hierarchies. A more effective model involves formalizing teacher input into institutional governance structures, such as curriculum review boards, observation rubric committees, or PD planning teams. Mechanisms like rotating representation ensure that participation is not monopolized by a small group of "preferred" teachers (Wang et al., 2022). Importantly, these forums should ensure transparent follow-up, so that teacher-generated ideas are visibly integrated into institutional policies or practices.

Training managers and teacher trainers in critical language awareness is essential to disrupt the reproduction of hegemonic norms. Leadership programs can address how policy language shapes teacher identity, how feedback discourse can be empowering or regulatory, and how to balance standardization with contextual flexibility. As Meighan (2025, p. 2) asserted, "Languages inform teachers' values, behaviors, and decisions, and are not disconnected from local political, sociocultural, and ecological contexts." Building on this, including modules on linguistic justice and equity in feedback can shift managerial culture toward one that recognizes the legitimacy of diverse approaches.

Beyond structural reforms, cultural change is necessary. This involves normalizing discussions about ideology and power in staffrooms, observation feedback, and PD sessions, so they are no longer seen as "political" in the pejorative sense, but as integral to professional practice (Giroux, 2020). Simple practices, such as managers modeling reflective talk, inviting multiple interpretations of "effective teaching," or sharing institutional decision-making rationales, help demystify authority and foster trust.

Finally, LTOs should explore innovative alternatives to traditional observation models. Approaches like NSO (which is still in its infancy) may gain more momentum and reframe observation as teacher-led inquiry, breaking the hierarchical pattern where the observer controls the discourse. Such approaches embody bottom-up PD, which allows teachers to position themselves as researchers of their own practice, while still engaging in supportive dialogue with colleagues.

In sum, addressing mesosystem issues of LaP in LTOs requires a multi-pronged approach: building awareness of the problem, ensuring role readiness before promotion, embedding teacher-led and collaborative structures, giving teachers a genuine voice, training leaders in critical language awareness, and experimenting with alternative observation and PD models. Without these steps, institutional language will continue to reinforce existing hierarchies; with them, it can become a vehicle for empowerment, diversity, and meaningful professional growth.

4 LaP in LTE Macrosystem

4.1 The Myth of Native Speakerism in LTE

This section aims to critically examine the ideology of native-speakerism in language teaching and its pervasive influence on LTE. Native speakerism, as a hegemonic discourse, constructs and privileges an idealized native speaker figure as the norm and ultimate model of language competence and pedagogical authority (Holliday, 2015). Such an ideology, embedded in broader structures of linguistic imperialism and standard language ideologies, has profound implications for how language teachers are perceived, evaluated, and trained within institutional and sociopolitical contexts (Uysal & Sah, 2024).

Before advancing this discussion, two clarifications are necessary. First (as discussed in the Preface of this Element, research on LTE is dominated by research on English), while the discourse of native speakerism has been increasingly acknowledged in relation to languages other than English

(LOTE), the vast majority of empirical studies to date have been situated within the field of ELT. As Ushioda (2017) notes, the global dominance of English has positioned ELT research as the de facto standard in language education and applied linguistics scholarship. This reflects more than just linguistic trends by actively reproducing underlying ideological hierarchies. Additionally, it is worth noting that many LOTE teachers are themselves expected to demonstrate proficiency in English, further reinforcing the centrality of English in discussions of native-speakerism. Consequently, the examples referenced throughout this section are primarily drawn from ELT.

Second, I take issue with the prevailing binary between native speaker teachers (NSTs) and non-native speaker teachers (NNSTs), a dichotomy that I consider both linguistically and ideologically problematic. A growing body of scholarship has highlighted the negative social, professional, and commercial consequences of this binary distinction (Mackenzie, 2021; Selvi, 2014). Recent scholarship has advanced *trans-speakerism* as a counter-ideology that rejects native–non-native binaries and centers diversity, equity, and inclusion (DEI) by valuing what teachers *are and can become* rather than what they are *not* (Hiratsuka et al., 2024). From my perspective, even the linguistic structure of the acronym "NNST" reflects a markedness that reinforces hierarchical thinking, a point echoing Chomskyan notions of marked and unmarked forms (Chomsky, 1993). The "non-" prefix inherently positions NNSTs as deviant from an idealized norm, perpetuating a deficit view. To counter this, I adopt the term "Global Speaker Teacher" (GST) in place of NNST. However, in this Element, I depart from Hiratsuka et al. (2024): Whereas global speakers/teachers of English (GSEs/GTEs) include both NSTs and NNSTs, I use GST solely for NNSTs[1] as a strategic, corrective remarking for historically marginalized teachers while recognizing *trans-speakerism* as the longer-term horizon for category abolition and system reform.

Efforts to critically examine the assumptions underpinning the binary distinction between so-called native and non-native speakers began to emerge sporadically in the 1980s, most notably in Paikeday's (1985) challenge to the legitimacy of the "native speaker" as a linguistic ideal. These critiques gained momentum in the 1990s, as scholars such as Rampton (1990), Davies (1991), and Phillipson (1992) interrogated the ideological foundations and sociopolitical implications of this constructed divide. Phillipson's (1992) seminal work on linguistic imperialism was particularly influential in exposing how privileging native speaker norms perpetuates inequalities in language education and reinforces global power

---

[1] **Note:** Although I use the term *Global Speaker Teacher* (GST) to challenge the deficit framing of the commonly used label *non-native speaker teacher* (NNST), this text uses NNST when referring to prior studies.

hierarchies. These early critiques laid the groundwork for the emergence of *native speakerism* as a named and theorized concept, which Holliday (2005) formalized as an ideology that idealizes native speakers while marginalizing others. This notion has since been expanded and refined by subsequent scholars (e.g., Houghton & Rivers, 2013; Swan et al., 2015; Lowe, 2020), who have examined its enduring impact on teacher identity, recruitment, and PD in language education. In this section, I build on these foundational critiques to argue that the native speaker construct is not only conceptually flawed but also ideologically charged, sustaining exclusionary practices within LTE.

The ideology of native speakerism is underpinned by a range of intersecting socio-political forces. Scholars have identified its foundations in linguicism (Dovchin, 2025), or discrimination based on language background (Rivers, 2018), as well as in forms of (neo-)racism that subtly reinforce racialized hierarchies in global language education (Holliday, 2015). Additionally, essentialist assumptions, which reduce individuals to fixed linguistic or cultural traits, further sustain this ideology (Holliday, 2005, 2021, 2022). More recently, researchers have argued that neoliberalism plays a central role in perpetuating native-speakerism by commodifying language and teaching identities in ways that privilege so-called native speakers in the global marketplace (Ruecker & Ives, 2015). Together, these forces construct and legitimize an exclusionary narrative that continues to shape hiring practices, professional recognition, and teacher identity within language education.

In the LTE ecosystem, native-speakerism functions as a deeply entrenched ideological construct, profoundly influencing perceptions of teacher identity, competence, and professional worth. Research investigating the presence and endurance of native speakerist ideology consistently demonstrates that it operates as a pervasive discourse shaping attitudes toward language teachers and educational practices (Holliday, 2005; Houghton & Bouchard, 2020; Lowe, 2020; Swan et al., 2015). This ideology elevates the figure of the native speaker as the ideal language user and educator, often based on essentialist assumptions about language proficiency and cultural authenticity. Such conceptualizations obscure the complex realities of multilingualism and the diverse linguistic repertoires that many language teachers bring to their practice. Moreover, native speakerism is intertwined with broader socio-political dynamics, including linguicism, (neo-) racism, and neoliberal agendas that commodify language teaching within globalized markets. As a result, native speakerism sustains exclusionary norms while weakening efforts to promote inclusivity and equity in LTE. The persistence of this ideology destabilizes the language teaching profession by fostering hierarchical distinctions that undervalue the skills and knowledge of the GSTs. Scholars argue that native speakerism is a harmful ideology that corrodes the foundations of LTE, reinforcing inequality and limiting the potential for culturally responsive and contextually grounded teacher development (Holliday, 2005; Houghton & Bouchard, 2020; Lowe, 2020; Swan et al., 2015). Although research findings on the priorities and roles of NST and GST have been mixed, greater attention should be given to GST in studies and LTE programs. This is particularly important because GSTs constitute approximately 80 percent of English teachers worldwide (Canagarajah, 2005), and this proportion can be reasonably extended to LOTE as well. Recognizing and integrating GSTs more prominently in research and training can help address their unique challenges and contributions, ultimately leading to more inclusive and effective language education practices globally.

The native-speakerism ideology is not only detrimental to GSTs, but it also adversely affects NSTs. Kamali and Nazari (2025) observe that NSTs are often positioned as symbolic assets or "brands" for their institutions primarily due to their racial and linguistic identities, rather than their pedagogical qualifications. Such essentialist positioning can be degrading, as it reduces complex professional identities to superficial markers and overshadows the teachers' actual expertise, training, and experience. This commodification of NSTs reinforces a racialized labor hierarchy within language education, ultimately undermining the professional integrity of all teachers and perpetuating inequitable structures within the global LTE landscape. Therefore, understanding the role of native-speakerism and actively working to reduce its impact within LTE is in the best interest of all teachers, regardless of whether they belong to the NST or GST group. A trans-speakerist lens, for instance, can make this symmetrical: It protects NSTs from commodification and GSTs from deficit framing by repositioning both as GSEs/GTEs whose legitimacy rests on professional conduct, contextual knowledge, and ethical practice (Hiratsuka et al., 2024). Effectively addressing native-speakerism thus entails adopting trans-speakerist elements in program designs and policies in LTE. The following section (4.2) addresses the political economy of colonial languages in Global South contexts, exploring how colonial histories continue to shape language ideologies, educational policies, and teacher identities in postcolonial settings.

4.2 The Political Economy in the Global South Colonial LTE

Education has always been a cradle of democracy, yet it is often one of the first things to come under attack when antidemocratic or authoritarian governments gain power (Hartnett & Naish, 1993). Time and again, when right-wing or conservative parties take office in influential countries such as the US, schools, and especially the people who teach in them, find themselves under intense pressure. Teachers and teacher educators are singled out, blamed for everything from slipping academic standards to moral decline and even wider economic struggles. A clear example is a recent call to abolish the US Department of Education altogether, sending a clear message that, for some leaders, education is not a fundamental right but an easy target for budget cuts. These populist governments often fuel what Ball (1990) calls a discourse of derision: A loud, repeated story in the media that paints public education as broken and teachers as its main problem. In this environment, teachers lose trust and freedom; they are told exactly what to teach, how to teach it, and how to prove it has been taught, leaving little room for their professional judgment or creativity (Hartnett & Naish, 1993). At its heart, this approach frames education as a managed investment in efficiency, viewing those devoted to teaching as administrative considerations rather than trusted collaborators in shaping society's future.

Political economy provides a precious framework for understanding how teacher education, including LTE, is shaped by broader political and economic forces. Education systems, and the training of educators within them, are deeply embedded in the power relations and resource distributions of society (Sah & Fang, 2025). Teacher education policies reflect more than technical decisions; they embody competing interests and ideological agendas that shape what knowledge is valued, how teachers are prepared, and who accesses PD opportunities (Apple, 2024). In recent decades, neoliberal reforms have increasingly influenced teacher education by emphasizing market principles such as accountability, standardization, and performance measurement (Ball, 2016; Neophytou, 2025). This has resulted in the commodification of LTE, where programs are pressured to produce measurable outcomes such as language-proficient and student-retention-oriented teachers, aligned with economic goals, sometimes at the expense of critical pedagogical approaches and the cultivation of democratic values (Apple, 2013).

LTE, in particular, faces unique challenges within this political economy framework. The global spread of English and other colonial languages (such as French and Spanish) is closely tied to economic globalization, positioning language teaching as a space where cultural, social, political, and economic interests converge – a context that calls for what Canagarajah (2025, p. 378) describes as a "decolonial turn" as an onto-epistemological concept. Policies often prioritize language skills that serve market needs, while sidelining critical, socially aware approaches to language teaching that foster intercultural understanding and social justice (Pennycook, 2001). Furthermore, access to quality LTE is often unequal, reinforcing broader social stratifications (Marginson, 2016). Understanding these dynamics encourages educators and policymakers to critically examine how political and economic structures shape teacher education, and to advocate for programs that balance accountability with empowering teachers as reflective, socially responsible practitioners (Ciampa & Reisboard, 2024). Ultimately, political economy highlights teacher education as a contested space where broader struggles over power, knowledge, and resources are enacted.

Understanding education, and particularly teacher education, through the lens of political economy reveals how deeply embedded power dynamics shape policies and daily classroom realities. Yet, when we bring this analysis into the context of the Global South, the picture becomes even more complex. As Hartnett and Naish (1993) insightfully remind us, "Educational change, therefore, has to be part of wider political change." (p. 345) Education systems cannot be separated from the historical, political, and economic structures that sustain inequality and colonial legacies. This is especially true in many Global South countries, where the persistent "Matthew Effect – the rich get richer and the poor get poorer" (Kubota, 2023, p. viii) plays out economically and in access to quality education and teacher training.

A key element to consider here is the ongoing influence of coloniality: "long-standing patterns of power that emerged as a result of colonialism, but that define culture, labor, intersubjective relations, and knowledge production well beyond the strict limits of colonial administrations" (Maldonado-Torres, 2007, p. 243). This means that even decades after formal colonial rule ended, educational systems often remain entangled with Eurocentric norms and values that continue to shape curricula, teacher education, and language policies. Decoloniality offers a path forward, challenging these dominant norms. As Gallien (2020) puts it, decoloniality is "a gesture that de-normalizes the normative, problematizes default positions, debunks the a-perspectival, destabilizes the structure" (p. 28), aiming to rehabilitate epistemologies repressed under coloniality. In LTE, this means moving beyond monolingual, native-speaker norms and embracing multilingual and culturally grounded pedagogies. Fang et al. (2022) argue that activating students' multilingual repertoires through translanguaging supports deeper learning, affirms learners' identities, and promotes decoloniality. Patel et al. (2023) envisioned a future in which English is "repositioned in models of education within which indigenous languages are increasingly valued" (p. 57), emphasizing the importance of multilingual education in postcolonial contexts. This approach counters the coloniality of language and aligns with equitable LTE that respects local knowledge and cultural diversity.

Finally, adopting dialogic and participatory research methods, as suggested by Bakhtin (1981), can empower language teachers as active agents rather than passive subjects, fostering more inclusive and contextually relevant educational development. Such approaches help dismantle colonial power relations embedded in research and policy-making. One such method within LTE is Language Teacher Action Research. Through iterative *plan–act–observe–reflect* cycles, teachers generate situated knowledge, implement it, document its impact, and channel findings upward into program and policy redesign. Recent syntheses in *The Routledge Handbook of Language Teacher Action Research* (Burns & Dikilitaş, 2024) show its effects on different layers of the LTE ecosystem, offering macrosystem levers to move beyond native-speakerist standards and toward equity. A clear example of using dialogic research is a recent collaborative research project by Dikilitaş et al. (2025) involving teacher-researchers from Argentina, India, and Turkey that illustrates the transformative potential of sustained engagement in teacher-led inquiry. This study employed an innovative, collaborative design in which all participants (Eryılmaz, Mukherjee, and Serra) acted as co-researchers, reflecting on their experiences through written, verbal, and dialogic communication. The findings revealed a gradual evolution in the participants' professional identities from initially experiencing teacher and researcher roles as separate or even conflicting, to developing what the authors term a "meta-identity" (p. 1): A reflexive, integrated awareness of these complementary identities evolving over time. Key factors that supported this transformation included sustaining curiosity, receiving appropriate support, recognizing the practical benefits of research, and gaining recognition within new professional communities. This example highlights how dialogic collaboration enriches teacher PD while challenging traditional hierarchical research dynamics, creating space for teachers' voices to shape knowledge production and educational practice in ways that are locally meaningful.

In sum, bringing together political economy and decolonial perspectives highlights LTE in the Global South as a vibrant space of dialogue, growth, and transformation. Advancing this work involves promoting equity, honoring diverse linguistic realities, and fostering education systems that are inclusive, democratic, and rooted in the lived experiences of communities.

4.3 Linguistic Capital and Market Logics in LTE

Within political economy, *linguistic capital* becomes central to understanding how LTE both reproduces and negotiates power relations embedded in wider educational and social structures. Building on Bourdieu's (1991) concept, linguistic capital highlights how particular ways of speaking are endowed with symbolic value that can translate into social mobility, professional recognition, and economic gain. This value is not inherent but constructed through interconnected practices of institutional norms and market logics that privilege dominant languages and standard varieties while marginalizing others. Within the LTE ecosystem (from classroom interactions to hiring, certification, and policy), these dynamics shape who is legitimized as a language teacher, whose linguistic practices are validated, and how multilingual realities are accommodated or suppressed within an unequal global order.

The idea of the free market, embedded in neoliberalism, which "proposes that human well-being can best be advanced by liberating individual entrepreneurial freedoms" (Harvey, 2005, p. 2), directly links to the notion of linguistic capital (Bourdieu, 1991). In a neoliberal context, languages and language skills become commodities that individuals can invest in and trade to gain social and economic advantage. This market-driven logic positions language learning and use as forms of capital accumulation, where proficiency in dominant or global languages (like English) yields symbolic and material benefits, reinforcing unequal access to employment opportunities within LTOs. For teachers from less privileged contexts, particularly in the Global South, this turns language education into an uncertain source of income, which can create further precarity (Walsh, 2019). Even when they do find jobs, they may remain vulnerable, since students and parents function as discerning consumers with varied "marketized choices" (Brown et al., 2010). As a result, teachers must constantly strive to meet these consumer demands, often at the cost of their own stability and autonomy. Many find themselves caught in "hamster wheel of precarious work" (Courtois & O'Keefe, 2015, p. 56), in which they endlessly cycle through short-term or insecure positions in order to survive within an education system shaped by neoliberal ideals.

This market logic, which is expanded to education in general and LTE in particular, considers that education is run like a business where the student is the customer, the teacher is the service provider, and learning is treated as a product (Gray & Block, 2013). Within this "market-driven economic system, you meet the demands of the consumer or you go out of business" (Clegg, 2000, p. 183). This view is in line with what Weber (1968) described as how Western society has increasingly moved toward rationalization, organizing systems that prioritize efficiency, calculability, predictability, and control. Efficiency means using the best methods to achieve a goal with minimal waste, exemplified by the assembly line, which streamlines tasks to save time and resources. Calculability focuses on measuring success through numbers, such as quantity produced or cost, often at the expense of quality. Predictability ensures that processes and outcomes remain consistent regardless of who performs the work, making the system "worker-proof" (Gray & Block, 2013, p. 122). Together, these elements create control, where both human oversight and technology maintain the smooth operation of the system. This control encourages individuals to follow routines that sustain the system, allowing only small adjustments but preventing any disruption. He further described how it devalues the individuals (in our case, teachers):

> The four characteristics of systems of organisation, making up a veritable template for uniformity, lead to a situation where human beings, as individuals, are important mainly for their instrumental value, and as a consequence, they are dehumanized and ultimately fall under the control of the bureaucracies which initially were created with the ostensible, though questionable, aim of making their lives easier (Gray & Block, 2013, p. 122).

Wallace (1991) argues that the development of LTE can be understood as unfolding in three main phases, each defined by a dominant model of what it means to be an effective teacher.

The first phase emphasized the *craft model*, where new teachers learn mainly through apprenticeship and practical classroom experience under the guidance of more experienced colleagues. This approach to teacher education is among the earliest and most traditional. However, as Wallace (1991) points out, it faced strong criticism after World War II for being overly conservative. Critics argued that its main goal was simply to train new teachers to copy the same routines and practices that were already in place, rather than encouraging fresh ideas or adapting to new educational needs. The second phase introduced the *applied science model*, positioning language teaching as a field that should draw on linguistic and pedagogical research to inform practice, with teacher education becoming more theoretical and research-based. However, not all teachers are researchers and are generally not very much interested in research, as they are mostly practice-oriented (Groothuijsen et al., 2019). The third phase brought forward the *reflective model*, which sees teachers not just as implementers of received knowledge but as active thinkers who examine and adapt their own teaching through critical reflection on their practice. However, the above-mentioned market-driven education climate often undermines this reflective ideal (Gray & Block, 2013). When education is shaped by market logic, teachers are pressured to deliver measurable results and meet consumer-like demands from students and parents, leaving little room for genuine reflection or experimentation. Instead of supporting teachers as thoughtful professionals who question and refine their practice, the system pushes them to stick to safe, standardized routines that can be easily packaged, marketed, and controlled. In this way, the promise of the reflective model is often overshadowed by the need to satisfy market expectations, keeping teachers on what Courtois and O'Keefe (2015) aptly call a "hamster wheel" of repetitive, controlled work that rarely allows space for meaningful growth or innovation.

One clear way linguistic capital shows up in today's LTE is through the rise of accreditation and certification bodies. This is especially visible in ELT, where obtaining a recognized certificate has become almost a must before a teacher can step into the classroom professionally. From my experience directing one of these courses, I see the practical side of such certifications. They are like a driver's license: A trusted proof that a person has met certain standards and can be relied upon. But at the same time, the way these certifications hold prestige, which translates to power, reinforces certain dominant systems and deserves a closer look.

Though the latest data can be hard to come by, we do know that a few key providers hold significant influence. For instance, the University of Cambridge's CELTA and Trinity College London's CertTESOL together authorize over 400 training centers around the world, training upwards of 10,000 teachers each year (Hobbs, 2013). When we zoom out to consider all TESOL programs, the picture becomes even bigger. Just in Canada and the US, there are more than 400 such courses (Barduhn & Johnson, 2009). Add to that, advanced certifications like DELTA and DipTESOL, aimed at more experienced teachers, and certificates for young learners, teaching IELTS, and so on.

What is striking about these certifications is how much they control access to ELT jobs. In many cases, if you do not hold one of these qualifications, you might not even get an interview or the chance to teach a demo lesson. Cambridge English (2018) confirms this, showing that CELTA is the most frequently requested qualification in ELT job ads worldwide:

> A study of 600 English language teaching job adverts in over 60 countries has revealed that Cambridge English's CELTA is the qualification most often requested by employers.
>
> CELTA is requested by 71.5 percent of employers in Europe, the Middle East and Africa, compared to just 23.6 percent asking for CELTA's nearest equivalent the Trinity CertTESOL. The data from the study further reveals that, in the UK, 88 percent of jobs that require an ELT qualification specifically ask for a CELTA qualification (Cambridge English, 2018, paras. 1–2).

The gatekeeping role of certifications like CELTA extends beyond signaling professional knowledge or skills; these qualifications also play a key role in shaping pathways into the ELT profession. They contribute to defining the expectations and benchmarks for entry, guiding how teaching expertise and language proficiency are recognized across diverse contexts. In doing so, they support a shared understanding of what counts as effective teaching, often drawing on globally accepted standards rooted in established traditions of English language education, like traditional approaches in teaching pronunciation (Sweeting & Carey, 2025). As these certifications are widely referenced in job advertisements and institutional hiring practices, they help shape the professional landscape and influence how teachers engage with career development opportunities around the world.

All in all, linguistic capital and market logics shape LTE today. While dominant discourses promise innovation and professional growth through reflection and research-informed practice, the reality for many teachers (especially those from less privileged contexts) is far more constrained. The commodification of language and teaching under neoliberalism turns education into a competitive marketplace where teachers must continuously perform, standardize, and reproduce existing norms to meet consumer expectations. Certifications such as CELTA and CertTESOL can intensify this practice. This, on the one hand, reinforces existing hierarchies of whose language and expertise count, and on the other, restricts teachers' capacity to act as reflective, critical professionals. As long as market-driven forces dictate the terms of teaching and learning, the transformative potential of linguistic capital in LTE remains limited; it, in effect, reproduces rather challenging social and educational inequalities.

4.4 Contesting Ownership in LTE

Multilingualism can be meaningfully understood through three interrelated ecological layers: the micro level of the individual, the meso level of institutions, and the macro level of society at large. This layered perspective is clearly reflected in the European Commission's (2007) definition, which describes multilingualism as "the ability of societies, institutions, groups and individuals to engage, on a regular basis, with more than one language in their day-to-day lives" (p. 6). Although multilingualism is not a new phenomenon and can be traced back to ancient texts which are written in different languages, it was long framed in negative terms by dominant power structures that sought to position monolingualism as the norm. As Cenoz and Gorter (2023, p. 9) point out:

> Up to the 1960s, multilingualism was generally associated with negative results in cognitive ability. Multilingual schoolchildren scored lower than monolinguals, particularly in verbal intelligence, but these tests often had serious methodological problems. The multilingual children tested in these studies were in contexts in which their first language was regarded as inferior in society and was not developed at school. Moreover, multilingual children often came from lower socioeconomic backgrounds than monolingual children.

This historical framing reveals how linguistic hierarchies and social power dynamics can distort perceptions of multilingualism, turning what is fundamentally a rich resource and cognitive strength into a presumed deficit. Today, however, there is growing recognition that multilingualism enriches both individuals and communities, opening doors to diverse ways of thinking, cultural exchange, and greater social cohesion that can be traced back to the influential work of Peal and Lambert (1962), who demonstrated that bilingual children outperformed their monolingual peers on a range of cognitive tasks, including both verbal and nonverbal measures. Despite this recognition, multilingual speakers (particularly those who engage in fluid, hybrid, or nonstandard language practices) continue to face translingual discrimination, a form of linguistic injustice whereby speakers are marginalized for not conforming to dominant language norms (Dovchin, 2022). This contradiction highlights the gap between ideology and lived experience. The commonly quoted saying: *A person who speaks with an accent knows one more language than you do*, captures the human reality behind the ecological layers of multilingualism: that each speaker's accent or code-switching is not a flaw, but tangible evidence of linguistic dexterity and openness to the world.

With the advent of the *multilingual turn* in education (Conteh & Meier, 2014; May, 2014), the rigid power structures that once shaped language education have increasingly been called into question. Before examining how this shift has occurred, it is useful to clarify the concept of a *turn*. According to Meier (2017), a *turn* "is a name given to a development that has established itself, or is in the process of establishing itself" (p. 132). Such shifts have long characterized the field; for example, the *cognitive turn* (Block, 2003) foregrounded cognitive processes in language learning. In contrast to this cognitive emphasis, the *social turn* gained momentum when Firth and Wagner (1997) critiqued dominant cognitivist paradigms by emphasizing the inherently social dimensions of language use. Their intervention paved the way for further reorientations in research, giving rise to subsequent shifts such as the *narrative turn* (Vásquez, 2011) and the *autoethnographic turn* (Mirhosseini, 2018), among others, which continue to broaden and deepen understandings of language and learning within diverse sociocultural contexts.

In LTE, the rise of multilingualism has significantly challenged and reshaped longstanding dynamics of linguistic power and imperialism. Historically, the dominance of English as a global lingua franca often privileged monolingual native speakers (especially those from Inner Circle countries; Kachru, 1986) as the default, desirable model for ELT (Phillipson, 1992). In ELT, for example, monolingual English speakers traditionally occupied the most prominent positions in global ELT markets (see the previous sections), reinforcing the idea that teaching English required native-speaker status and, implicitly, a single-language worldview.

However, this narrative has been steadily disrupted by the increasing visibility and legitimacy of multilingual English teachers around the world. At the micro-individual level, multilingual educators bring a heightened metalinguistic awareness and a deeper understanding of language learning processes. Because they have personally navigated multiple linguistic and cultural systems, they are often better equipped to empathize with learners' challenges and to draw on diverse linguistic repertoires as pedagogical resources (Dewaele & Wei, 2012; Llurda & Calvet-Terré, 2025). Their experience as language learners themselves allows them to model effective strategies and foster more inclusive, multilingual classrooms.

At the meso-institutional level, LTE programs are progressively recognizing the value of multilingual competence. Many LTE programs now actively recruit and prepare teachers who can draw on multiple languages and cultural frames of reference. For example, at our teacher education center, all trainees we have trained to date are multilingual. Similarly, at the language school of the university where I work, every member of the teaching staff is multilingual, reflecting the growing recognition of linguistic diversity as a valuable asset in English language education. This shift reflects a broader commitment to embracing linguistic diversity as an asset, rather than viewing it as a hindrance to "standard" language teaching. By integrating multilingual pedagogies, institutions challenge outdated native-speakerist ideologies and help future teachers support learners in leveraging their full linguistic repertoires (Cenoz & Gorter, 2023).

At the macro-societal level, the growing presence of multilingual language teachers has contributed to broader social respect for linguistic diversity and has challenged monolingual hierarchies (Sperti, 2025). In many communities, multilingual educators are increasingly recognized not only as highly qualified professionals but also as cultural mediators who embody the complex realities of global language use. As a result, the symbolic power of dominant languages is being redefined to accommodate diverse accents, varieties, and translanguaging practices (see Section 2).

Despite these encouraging signs of change, we know that monolingualism still quietly shapes how many people think about language teaching, and old habits do not disappear overnight. If we truly want to move beyond this, we need to make room for real multilingual practices in our LTE programs (Kamali & Alpat, 2025). This means helping future teachers see the rich possibilities that multiple languages bring to the classroom and giving them the tools and confidence to value what learners already know. It is an ongoing effort, but if we keep this conversation alive, we can take meaningful steps toward a more inclusive and realistic vision of language education.

4.5 Addressing Macrosystem Issues of LaP in the Sociopolitics of LTE

At the macrosystem scale, LaP is produced in arenas far larger than any single program: state policy, global markets, credentialing regimes, scholarly canons, media discourses, and enduring colonialities. These forces sediment into norms that privilege "standard" varieties and native-speaker ideals, shaping who is authorized to teach and what counts as legitimate knowledge in LTE (Holliday, 2015; Phillipson, 1992; Uysal & Sah, 2024). Addressing the problem, therefore, means intervening in the sociopolitical infrastructures that manufacture linguistic inequality.

First, ministries, professional councils, and international frameworks should move beyond monolingual standardization by adopting multilingual descriptors and outcome statements that validate locally legitimate varieties and translanguaging as pedagogical resources (Cenoz & Gorter, 2023; Fang et al., 2022). Antidiscrimination provisions against linguicism and accentism ought to be written into teacher licensing, public hiring, and migration rules to prevent native-speaker proxies from functioning as de facto barriers (Rivers, 2018; Uysal & Sah, 2024).

Second, neoliberal governance narrows teacher agency by tethering funding, ranking, and employment to audit-friendly metrics and marketized "quality," converting linguistic capital into an exclusionary filter (Bourdieu, 1991; Apple, 2013; Ball, 2016; Gray & Block, 2013). System-level remedies include funding formulas that reward equity and multilingual inclusion, not just throughput and test yield; portability of credentials across borders without native-speaker stipulations; and labor protections that reduce the precarity that disproportionately affects globally mobile teachers (Courtois & O'Keefe, 2015; Walsh, 2019).

Third, standardized examinations and teacher credentials operate as gatekeepers that naturalize a narrow model of correctness (Ruecker & Ives, 2015). Regulators and awarding bodies should revise competencies to foreground interactional competence, intelligibility across varieties, and critical language awareness, decoupling "quality" from monolingual norms (Cenoz & Gorter, 2023). Public reporting on the linguistic ideologies embedded in rubrics – what is counted, and who benefits – creates democratic oversight of these markets (Gray & Block, 2013).

Fourth, Colonial epistemologies persist when LTE research, journals, and curricula center Inner-Circle literatures and erase Global South scholarship and practitioner knowledge (Canagarajah, 2025; Maldonado-Torres, 2007; Pennycook, 2001). Decolonial moves include multilingual publishing policies, editorial diversification, open-access mandates for publicly funded work, and recognition of teacher-led, participatory inquiries as legitimate knowledge production (e.g., Dikilitaş et al., 2025). Such reweighting redistributes epistemic authority and reframes teachers as coproducers rather than consumers of theory.

Fifth, raciolinguistic ideologies circulate through news, advertising, and platformed influencer culture, branding certain norms as employable and others as suspect (Dovchin, 2025; Holliday, 2015). Counter-discursive strategies (such as public campaigns on linguistic citizenship, language-rights charters in education, and media guidelines against accent shaming) help reshape common sense about legitimacy and expertise. As part of these counter-discursive strategies, institutionalizing trans-speakerism as a system principle that replaces native/non-native binaries with GSE/GTE framing and DEI-aligned professionalism would constitute a robust policy lever.

Taken together, these interventions reorient LTE's sociopolitics from deficit and gatekeeping to equity and recognition. The task is a redistribution of symbolic and material power: redefining which varieties are legitimate, who counts as a qualified teacher, and whose knowledge anchors our canons. When policy, credentialing, political economy, scholarly practice, and public discourse align around multilingual, decolonial commitments, the LTE macrosystem becomes an enabling environment for linguistic justice rather than an engine of exclusion (Dovchin, 2025; Holliday, 2015; Phillipson, 1992; Uysal & Sah, 2024).

5 Future Trajectories of LaP in the LTE Ecosystem

In this final section, I will discuss the future trajectories for LaP in the LTE Ecosystem based on the present evidence. To do so, I rely on futurology, the systematic exploration of alternative futures and the choices that shape them, built on three premises: The future is not predictable, multiple futures exist, and present decisions can influence outcomes (Amara, 1981). I discuss three types of futures in this discipline. However, as artificial intelligence (AI) plays a significant role in our future, I will first discuss the (positive) impact of AI on LaP in different layers of the LTE Ecosystem and then turn to the types of futures envisioned for it.

5.1 The Impact of AI on LaP in LTE Ecosystem

To start this section, I thought, what is better than asking ChatGPT to give me an answer about what it can do for language power dynamics in LTE? Therefore,

I gave its free version this prompt: How will AI affect language power in LTE in the microsystem, mesosystem, and macrosystem? This is the reply:

> In the future, AI will reconfigure language power across all three layers of the LTE ecosystem in increasingly productive ways. At the microsystem, advances in automated writing evaluation, ASR, and intelligent tutoring will deliver more personalized scaffolding, minimize feedback delays, and free mentors' time for higher-order, dialogic engagement – enhancing novice teachers' capacity to experiment, reflect, and iterate with confidence. At the mesosystem (LTOs and departments), AI will be able to detect program-level patterns – such as recurring challenges in lesson plans or practicum reflections – providing data to guide targeted professional development and enabling more consistent formative assessment through transparently aligned rubrics. At the macrosystem, next-generation machine translation, accessibility features, and culturally adapted AI models will broaden participation beyond dominant linguistic centers, while human-centred governance and forward-looking accreditation standards will embed safeguards that preserve teacher and learner agency.

Although my discussion draws on these responses, numerous additional issues need consideration, which, in turn, have prompted scholars to exercise caution in adopting AI-generated ideas, as emphasized in the US standards body's *AI Risk Management Framework* (National Institute of Standards and Technology [NIST], 2023). Recent work in initial LTE also underscores this caution: While generative AI can broaden access to resources and feedback, its uptake demands critical mediation by teacher educators to avoid reproducing false information, dominant language ideologies, and to develop clear, ethical replies (Moorhouse & Kohnke, 2024).

The following section examines the ways in which AI contributes to managing LaP within the LTE ecosystem (see Figure 2).[2]

5.1.1 AI and LTE Microsystem

At the individual level, AI tools can act as personalized PD partners (Copur-Gencturk et al., 2024). Language teachers can use AI to rehearse lessons, generate context-specific examples, or explore alternative ways to explain complex concepts. This self-directed engagement fosters pedagogical confidence and deepens content mastery, reducing reliance on externally dictated materials and teaching scripts. For example, a teacher might use an AI-driven language model to explore culturally relevant idioms or authentic materials drawn from the target language's contemporary use. By curating these

---

[2] **Note:** Given that many of these applications are already operational and practicable, the discussion is articulated in the present tense.

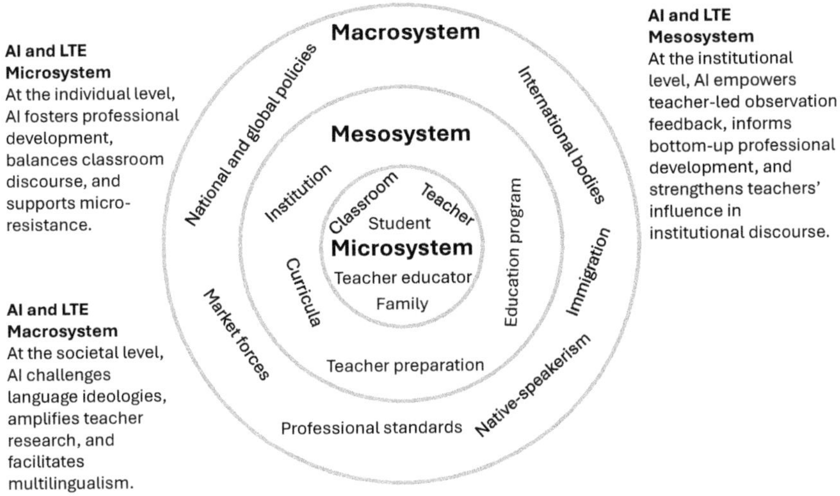

Language as Power in the Language Teacher Education Ecosystem 57

AI and LTE Microsystem
At the individual level, AI fosters professional development, balances classroom discourse, and supports micro-resistance.

AI and LTE Macrosystem
At the societal level, AI challenges language ideologies, amplifies teacher research, and facilitates multilingualism.

AI and LTE Mesosystem
At the institutional level, AI empowers teacher-led observation feedback, informs bottom-up professional development, and strengthens teachers' influence in institutional discourse.

Macrosystem — National and global policies, International bodies, Immigration, Native-speakerism, Professional standards, Market forces, Curricula, Institution, Education program

Mesosystem — Classroom, Teacher

Microsystem — Student, Teacher educator, Family, Teacher preparation

Figure 2 How AI can balance language power in the LTE ecosystem

themselves, teachers reassert control over lesson content to ensure it aligns with both curriculum goals and their own pedagogical values (Ning et al., 2024). This self-generated material becomes a form of epistemic authority (Zagzebski, 2012), that is, knowledge created and validated by the teacher, not imposed by external evaluators.

In classroom discourse, AI can help teachers design the interactional architecture (Seedhouse, 2004) of the classroom in a way that encourages more equitable participation and richer student engagement. AI-powered transcription and analysis tools can, for instance, identify participation imbalances, question types, and opportunities for student-led dialogue. Teachers can then intentionally shift from a heavily teacher-led pattern to more dialogic talk, amplifying both their own facilitation skills and student voice (Boyd, 2023). Furthermore, AI can assist in strategic language planning, enabling teachers to preplan questions, prompts, and real-time adaptations in multiple languages. This supports translanguaging practices, allowing teachers to validate students' linguistic repertoires and subtly resist monolingual norms embedded in many institutional policies (Hofer & Jessner, 2025).

The microsystem is also the site for micro-resistance: Small, everyday acts that challenge restrictive norms without overt confrontation (see Section 2 for more information). AI can bolster these acts by giving teachers resources, confidence, and linguistic agility. For instance, teachers can use AI to create counter-narratives to institutional scripts, framing lesson objectives in ways that affirm student identities or alternative perspectives. Also, AI-assisted content generation can help teachers weave in culturally relevant humor, which fosters rapport and disrupts the formality of hierarchical teacher–student relationships. In addition, AI-powered translation and corpus tools can supply precise, context-sensitive vocabulary across languages, enabling teachers and students to fluidly shift between linguistic codes. This improves comprehension and affirms the legitimacy of students' home languages in academic spaces, subtly resisting deficit views of multilingualism.

By combining AI's analytical capacities with their own pedagogical judgment, teachers can redefine classroom norms from the ground up in the LTE microsystem. They can set the tone for inclusive, dialogic, and linguistically diverse learning environments. In doing so, they can actively shape their practice to reflect their values and expertise. In short, AI's role at the LTE microsystem level is to amplify teacher agency, providing the tools, insights, and creative possibilities that allow teachers to enact and sustain professional autonomy in the most immediate arena of their work.

5.1.2 AI and LTE Mesosystem

In the LTE mesosystem, AI can help teachers regain control through self-analysis tools. Observation cycles have long been a site of institutional control. Standardized checklists, prescriptive rubrics, and managerial feedback discourse can limit teacher voice and reinforce dominant pedagogical norms (Pallas & Touloukian, 2024). AI-driven observation and feedback tools such as classroom audio/video analysis systems, speech recognition for discourse patterns, and AI-assisted lesson annotation (Donmez, 2024) offer opportunities for teacher-led interpretation rather than compliance monitoring.

For example, an AI system could automatically transcribe a lesson and highlight patterns in teacher talk time, questioning strategies, or wait time. Rather than an observer dictating improvement areas, the teacher could explore these data independently or collaboratively with a peer, reframing the post-observation meeting as a dialogic inquiry space. This reduces the asymmetry where the observer controls the narrative and allows teachers to set their own developmental agendas, reclaiming decision-making power about what constitutes "good" practice (Boyd & Markarian, 2011).

AI can also store teacher-made evidence banks, such as samples of practice, contextual challenges, and student responses, that inform feedback discussions. By grounding the dialogue in teacher-selected data rather than observer-selected evidence, AI enables teachers to steer the focus toward their professional priorities. This aligns with sociocultural perspectives on teacher development, which emphasize self-regulation and agency (Poehner & Lantolf, 2024).

Regarding the PDs, workshops often reflect institutional agendas: new curricular requirements, standardized assessments, or strategic partnerships with publishers. While these serve legitimate organizational goals, they may marginalize teacher-identified needs. AI can invert this design process by aggregating and analyzing teacher-generated data, for example, feedback surveys, reflective journals, and student performance patterns, to inform workshop planning. For instance, an AI platform could detect recurrent themes across teachers' reflections (e.g., challenges with emergent multilingual learners or integrating authentic materials) and suggest workshop topics accordingly. This data-driven, bottom-up, self-directed planning (Koay, 2023) can persuade institutional managers to prioritize sessions that address real classroom complexities rather than abstract compliance metrics.

During workshops, AI-powered tools (such as interactive simulations or adaptive resource generators) can personalize tasks to the teacher's context. This reduces the "one-size-fits-all" nature of many institutional trainings and strengthens teachers' perception that professional learning is relevant, context-responsive, and co-constructed.

In the mesosystem, power is not just about control over classroom practice but also influence over institutional discourse (Freed, 2015) – the policies, guidelines, and norms that define professional legitimacy. AI can assist teachers in gathering institutionally legible evidence (quantitative trends, qualitative excerpts, or comparative analyses) that bolsters their voices in curriculum committees, quality assurance meetings, and accreditation reviews. When teachers can present data that are both context-rich and analytically robust, they shift from being data subjects to data authors, changing the research process into autoethnographic research (Yazan, 2024).

Ultimately, AI in the institutional mesosystem can function as a discursive equalizer. By supporting teacher autonomy in observation feedback and PD, AI helps redistribute epistemic authority from the institution to the practitioner, and enables teachers to participate as active agents rather than passive recipients of institutional knowledge.

5.1.3 AI and LTE Macrosystem

Standard language ideology promotes the belief that a single, standardized variety of a language is inherently superior and that teachers must model it (Burns, 2025). Native speakerism further positions individuals with a certain birthplace or cultural background as the ideal teachers (Selvi et al., 2024). AI can help dismantle these hierarchies by generating instructional materials in multiple regional and social varieties of a language (Swargiary, 2024), whether that be dialectal Arabic, regional varieties of Spanish, or diverse accents in Mandarin.

Speech synthesis tools can be trained on local and community voices, normalizing them as legitimate classroom models. Multilingual text generation can likewise produce parallel lesson materials that valorize nonstandard varieties. In doing so, teachers gain data-driven evidence to resist policies or assessment rubrics that privilege a narrow "prestige" variety. Many LTE curricula, methods, and textbooks still reflect colonial power structures, where methods, research, and standards originate in former imperial centers (Kumar, 2018). AI can shift this by giving teachers tools to translate, publish, and disseminate locally produced scholarship across languages and platforms. For example, a teacher-researcher in Morocco can use AI-assisted translation to make Amazigh-French bilingual pedagogy research accessible to Arabic-speaking colleagues, or to share findings with international audiences. This bypasses linguistic barriers that have historically limited GSTs (see Section 4 for the term) influence in global discourse, repositioning them as knowledge producers rather than consumers.

Accreditation systems often reward teachers for mastering and transmitting market-valued linguistic capital (Skourdoumbis & Madkur, 2020), such as the "business register" of Japanese or the formal variety of German, while sidelining community or heritage varieties. AI-powered analytics can help teachers document learning gains from diverse linguistic practices. For example, they can integrate dialectal input in early literacy or bilingual glossing in heritage language maintenance (Kupolati, 2024). By producing quantifiable results that accreditation bodies recognize, teachers can defend pedagogies that might otherwise be undervalued, aligning market logics with socially responsive practices.

AI can operationalize multilingual pedagogies by making it easy to integrate multiple languages into lesson planning, assessment, and resource creation (Kuzu et al., 2025). Teachers can use cross-lingual search, AI-curated multilingual reading lists, or machine translation to position multiple languages as co-resources for learning, not just as bridges to a dominant language. By embedding these practices visibly in materials and assessments, teachers model a worldview in which linguistic diversity is an asset, challenging monolingual norms in LTE at the policy and cultural levels.

Overall, at the macrosystem level, AI can be more than a tool for efficiency; it can be an instrument of ideological disruption and social justice (Graham & Hopkins, 2021). By supporting teachers in contesting SLI and native speakerism, amplifying Global South research, reframing accreditation priorities, and embedding multilingual practices, AI helps redistribute power in LTE toward those most connected to local classrooms and communities. This enables teachers of all languages (not only English) to shape the cultural and political narratives that govern their profession.

5.2 The 3Ps of LaP Future in the LTE Ecosystem

Amara (1981), in describing the future in the science of futurology, introduced three types of futures as follows (see also Bell, 1998; Börjeson et al., 2006):

- Possible futures: Everything that *could* happen, constrained only by what is physically/technically/socially conceivable.
- Probable futures: What is *likely* to happen if current trends continue.
- Preferable futures: What we *want* to happen.

Applying these three Ps (possible, probable, and preferable futures) to the LTE ecosystem, which is deeply shaped by sociopolitical ideologies, market logics, accreditation frameworks, and shifting technological landscapes, offers a structured lens to explore how LaP might evolve within this complex ecology.

5.2.1 Possible Futures

Possible futures encompass the broadest set of trajectories, those that can be imagined within physical, social, and political constraints. In the LTE ecosystem, these include scenarios where AI-mediated technology radically alters the value of certain linguistic capitals, or where multilingual LTE becomes the norm due to policy shifts in international accreditation bodies. Other possibilities include intensified commercialization of "standard" language varieties through corporate testing regimes, or conversely, the emergence of decentralized, teacher-led certification systems that value local linguistic repertoires. The possible future space also includes more disruptive shifts, such as geopolitical changes that reposition dominant languages in global education, or climate-induced migration patterns that transform linguistic demographics in LTE programs. While not all possible futures are equally likely, exploring them helps identify overlooked threats and opportunities.

5.2.2 Probable Futures

Probable futures represent what is likely to occur if current trends continue without significant intervention. At present, the LTE ecosystem is shaped by the persistence of SLI, native-speakerist hiring preferences, and accreditation systems that embed monolingual norms. The probable trajectory, therefore, points toward further entrenchment of these hierarchies, albeit reframed through digital and AI-mediated platforms. For example, AI-driven observation tools may standardize feedback discourse even more tightly, reinforcing top-down professional regulation. International LTE markets are also likely to continue privileging English and other dominant languages, with world Englishes discourse coexisting uneasily alongside global assessment regimes. This probable path risks deepening inequities between educators in the Global North and South, as access to accredited programs, recognized qualifications, and linguistic prestige remains uneven.

5.2.3 Preferable Futures

Preferable futures refer to what we want to happen. Here, a preferable future would see the LTE ecosystem decentering monolingualism and re-centering multilingual, locally responsive pedagogies. This could involve policy-level shifts in accreditation standards to value multiple linguistic repertoires; teacher-led observation frameworks that redistribute discursive authority; and research agendas that foreground voices from marginalized linguistic communities. Preferable futures would also utilize AI to challenge conformity to dominant norms and to reveal and legitimize diverse forms of linguistic capital, enabling teacher educators and trainees to resist homogenizing pressures. Such a trajectory would promote equitable participation, which enables teachers in varied geopolitical contexts to shape the narratives of what counts as "quality" and "justice" in LTE.

In summary, the futurological analysis underscores that while probable futures may lean toward the continued dominance of SLI, the space of possible futures includes transformative scenarios – some beneficial, some detrimental. The challenge for LTE stakeholders lies in deliberately steering toward preferable futures, where it moves toward equity rather than exclusion. This requires conscious, multilevel interventions, such as policy reform, institutional redesign, and grassroots professional activism, to ensure the ecosystem's evolution aligns with socially just goals. As Amara (1981) reminds us, futures are not simply predicted; they are created through deliberate choice and sustained action. Therefore, all of us who inhabit this ecosystem are responsible for freeing it from linguistic hegemony; not more contests for power, but a just peace in which every voice is heard. As Rumi (n.d.), my source of inspiration, reminds us:

تو مگو همه به جنگند و ز ِصلح من چه آید
تو یکی نه‌ای هزاری تو چراغِ خود برافروز
Say not, "All are at war; what use is my peace?"
Thou art not one but a thousand; kindle thine own light.[3]

---

[3] Translation mine.

References

Aguiar, O. G., Mortimer, E. F., & Scott, P. (2010). Learning from and responding to students' questions: The authoritative and dialogic tension. *Journal of Research in Science Teaching: The Official Journal of the National Association for Research in Science Teaching, 47*(2), 174–193. https://doi.org/10.1002/tea.20315.

Alexander, R. J. (2017). *Towards dialogic teaching: Rethinking classroom talk* (5th ed.). Dialogos.

Allwright, D. (2005). Developing principles for practitioner research: The case of exploratory practice. *The Modern Language Journal, 89*(3), 353–366. https://doi.org/10.1111/j.1540-4781.2005.00310.x.

Amara, R. (1981, February). The futures field: Searching for definitions and boundaries. *The Futurist, 15*(1), 25–29.

Apple, M. W. (2013). *Knowledge, power, and education*. Routledge.

Apple, M. W. (2024). Sites of educational conflict. *Educational Policy, 38*(2), 548–556. https://doi.org/10.1177/08959048221120275.

Asher, J. J. (1969). The total physical response approach to second language learning. *Modern Language Journal, 53*(1), 3–17. https://doi.org/10.2307/322091.

Bailey, K. M. (2006). *Language teacher supervision: A case-based approach*. Cambridge University Press.

Baker, C. (2001). *Foundations of bilingual education and bilingualism* (3rd ed.). Multilingual Matters.

Bakhtin, M. M. (1981). *The dialogic imagination: Four essays* (M. Holquist, Ed.; C. Emerson & M. Holquist, Trans.). University of Texas Press.

Bakker, C., & Ter Avest, I. (2019). Teacher training for religious education: Engaging academics through the dialogical self theory. *Transformation in Higher Education, 4*(1), 1–9. https://doi.org/10.4102/the.v4i0.50.

Ball, S. J. (1990). *Politics and policy making in education*. Routledge.

Ball, S. J. (2003). The teacher's soul and the terrors of performativity. *Journal of Education Policy, 18*(2), 215–228. https://doi.org/10.1080/0268093022000043065.

Ball, S. J. (2016). Neoliberal education? Confronting the slouching beast. *Policy futures in education, 14*(8), 1046–1059. https://doi.org/10.1177/1478210316664259.

Bao, D. (2023). *Silence in English language pedagogy*. Cambridge University Press.

References

Baratta, A. (2018). 'I speak how I speak': A discussion of accent and identity within teachers of ELT. In B. Yazan, N. Rudolph (Eds.), *Criticality, teacher identity, and (in)equity in English language teaching: Issues and implications* (pp. 163–178). Springer. https://doi.org/10.1007/978-3-319-72920-6_11.

Barduhn, S., & Johnson, J. (2009). Certification and professional qualifications. In A. Burns & J. C. Richards (Eds.), *The Cambridge guide to second language teacher education* (pp. 59–65). Cambridge University Press.

Barkhuizen, G. (2017). *Reflections on language teacher identity research*. Routledge.

Beck, D., & Spencer, A. (2025). (Un) Funny against all odds: The changing landscape of humour in politics. *Alternatives, 50*(1), 3–17. https://doi.org/10.1177/03043754241290911.

Beiler, I. R., & Villacañas de Castro, L. S. (2025). Translanguaging and culturally sustaining pedagogies: A mutually dependent relationship? *Foreign Language Annals, 58*(1), 159–181. https://doi.org/10.1111/flan.12791.

Bell, W. (1998). Making people responsible: The possible, the probable, and the preferable. *American Behavioral Scientist, 42*(3), 323–339.

Bhabha, H. K. (1994). *The location of culture*. Routledge.

Billig, M. (2005). *Laughter and ridicule: Towards a social critique of humour*. Sage.

Block, D. (2003). *The social turn in second language acquisition*. Edinburgh University Press.

Blommaert, J. (2010). *The sociolinguistics of globalization*. Cambridge University Press.

Borg, S. (2015). *Teacher cognition and language education: Research and practice*. Bloomsbury.

Börjeson, L., Höjer, M., Dreborg, K. H., Ekvall, T., & Finnveden, G. (2006). Scenario types and techniques: Towards a user's guide. *Futures, 38*(7), 723–739. https://doi.org/10.1016/j.futures.2005.12.002.

Bouchard, J. (2020). The resilience of native-speakerism: A realist perspective. In Houghton, S.A., Bouchard, J. (Eds.), *Native-speakerism: Its resilience and undoing* (pp. 17–45). Springer Singapore. https://doi.org/10.1007/978-981-15-5671-5_2.

Bourdieu, P. (1991). *Language and symbolic power*. Harvard University Press.

Boyd, M. P. (2023). Teacher talk that supports student thinking and talking together: Three markers of a dialogic instructional stance. *Learning, Culture and Social Interaction, 39*, 100695. https://doi.org/10.1016/j.lcsi.2023.100695.

Boyd, M. P., & Markarian, W. C. (2011). Dialogic teaching: Talk in service of a dialogic stance. *Language and Education, 25*(6), 515–534. https://doi.org/10.1080/09500782.2011.597861.

Broadwell, M. M. (1969). Teaching for learning (XVI). *The Gospel Guardian, 20*(41), 1–3.

Bronfenbrenner, U. (1979). *The ecology of human development.* Harvard University Press.

Bronfenbrenner, U. (1993). The ecology of cognitive development: Research models and fugitive findings. In Wozniak, R. H. & Fischer, K. W. (Eds.), *Development in context: Acting and thinking in specific environments* (pp. 3–44). Hillsdale, NJ: Erlbaum.

Brown, P., Lauder, H., & Ashton, D. (2010). *The global auction: The broken promises of education, jobs, and incomes.* Oxford University Press.

Brown, P., & Levinson, S. C. (1978). Universals in language usage: Politeness phenomena. In E. N. Goody (Eds.), *Questions and politeness: Strategies in social interaction* (pp. 56–311). Cambridge University Press.

Burbules, N. (1993). *Dialogue in teaching: Theory and practice.* Teachers College Press.

Burns, K. E. (2025). Challenging standard language ideology in L2 learning contexts for endangered and minority languages. In W. Wei & J. Schnell (Eds.), *The Routledge handbook of endangered and minority languages* (pp. 274–287). Routledge.

Burns, A., & Dikilitaş, K. (Eds.). (2024). *The Routledge handbook of language teacher action research.* Taylor & Francis.

Butler, N. (2013). Joking aside: Theorizing laughter in organizations. *Culture and Organization, 21*(1), 42–58. https://doi.org/10.1080/14759551.2013.799163.

Cambridge English. (2018, April 3). *Three quarters of ELT jobs ask for Cambridge CELTA.* Cambridge Assessment English. www.cambridgeenglish.org/news/view/three-quarters-of-elt-jobs-ask-for-cambridge-celta/.

Canagarajah, A. S. (1999). *Resisting linguistic imperialism in English teaching.* Oxford University Press.

Canagarajah, A. S. (2002). *A geopolitics of academic writing.* University of Pittsburgh Press.

Canagarajah, S. (Ed.) (2005). *Reclaiming the local in language policy and practice.* Lawrence Erlbaum.

Canagarajah, S. (2013). Theorizing a competence for translingual practice at the contact zone. In S. May (Ed.), *The multilingual turn: Implications for SLA, TESOL and bilingual education* (pp. 78–102). Routledge.

Canagarajah, S. (2018). Translingual practice as spatial repertoires: Expanding the paradigm beyond structuralist orientations. *Applied linguistics, 39*(1), 31–54. https://doi.org/10.1093/applin/amx041.

Canagarajah, S. (2025). Diversifying "English" at the decolonial turn. *TESOL Quarterly, 59*(1), 378–389. https://doi.org/10.1002/tesq.3306.

Carless, D., & Boud, D. (2018). The development of student feedback literacy: Enabling uptake of feedback. *Assessment & Evaluation in Higher Education, 43*(8), 1315–1325. https://doi.org/10.1080/02602938.2018.1463354.

Cenoz, J., & Gorter, D. (2023). Multilingualism. In L. Wei, Z. Hua, & J. Simpson (Eds.), *The Routledge handbook of applied linguistics* (pp. 7–18). Routledge.

Cervantes-Soon, C. G. (2025). When silence speaks: Power, marginalization, and Latinx immigrant students in dual language classrooms. *Journal of Latinos and Education*, 1–20. https://doi.org/10.1080/15348431.2025.2497525.

Chan, P. H., & Aubrey, S. (2024). Strengthening teacher–student rapport through the practice of guided dialogue journaling. *RELC Journal, 55*(1), 179–189. https://doi.org/10.1177/00336882211044874.

Chomsky, N. (1993). *Lectures on government and binding: The Pisa lectures* (No. 9). Walter de Gruyter.

Ciampa, K., & Reisboard, D. (2024). Empowering teacher educators: Advancing culturally responsive practices through professional development. *Action in Teacher Education, 46*(4), 350–371. https://doi.org/10.1080/01626620.2024.2357088.

Clegg, A. J. (2000). Market-driven education. In S. Hakim, D. J. Ryan, & J. C. Stull (Eds.), *Restructuring education: Innovations and evaluations of alternative systems* (pp. 183–195). Greenwood Publishing Group.

Conteh, J., & Meier, G. (Eds.). (2014). *The multilingual turn in languages education: Opportunities and challenges*. Multilingual Matters.

Copland, F. (2012). Legitimate talk in feedback conferences. *Applied linguistics, 33*(1), 1–20. https://doi.org/10.1093/applin/amr040.

Copland, F., & Donaghue, H. (2019). Post observation feedback. In S. Walsh & S. Mann (Eds.), *The Routledge handbook of English language teacher education* (pp. 402–416). Routledge.

Copland, F., & Neokleous, G. (2011). L1 to teach L2: Complexities and contradictions. *ELT Journal 65*(3), 270–280. https://doi.org/10.1093/elt/ccq047.

Copur-Gencturk, Y., Li, J., & Atabas, S. (2024). Improving teaching at scale: can AI be incorporated into professional development to create interactive, personalized learning for teachers?. *American Educational Research Journal, 61*(4), 767–802. https://doi.org/10.3102/00028312241248514.

Courtois, A. D. M., & O'Keefe, T. (2015). Precarity in the ivory cage: Neoliberalism and casualisation of work in the Irish higher education sector. *Journal for critical education policy studies, 13*(1), 43–66.

Cummins, J. (2000). Academic language learning, transformative pedagogy, and information technology: Towards a critical balance. *TESOL Quarterly, 34*(3), 537–548. https://doi.org/10.2307/3587742.

Daoud, S., & Kasztalska, A. (2025). Exploring native-speakerism in teacher job recruitment discourse through legitimation code theory: The case of the United Arab Emirates. *Language Teaching Research, 29*(2), 786–806. https://doi.org/10.1177/13621688211066883.

Davies, A. (1991). *The native speaker in applied linguistics*. Edinburgh University Press.

De Costa, P. I. (2025). Pedagogizing identity: Why it matters, and where do we go from here?. *RELC Journal, 56*(1), 214–218. https://doi.org/10.1177/00336882251321184.

del Valle, J. (2014). The politics of normativity and globalization: Which Spanish in the classroom? *The Modern Language Journal, 98*(1), 358–372. https://doi.org/10.1111/j.1540-4781.2014.12066.x.

Dewaele, J. M., & Wei, L. (2012). Multilingualism, empathy and multicompetence. *International Journal of Multilingualism, 9*(4), 352–366. https://doi.org/10.1080/14790718.2012.714380.

Diaz, A., Cochran, K., & Karlin, N. (2016). The influence of teacher power on English language learners' self-perceptions of learner empowerment. *College Teaching, 64*(4), 158–167. https://doi.org/10.1080/87567555.2015.1126801.

Dikilitaş, K., Eryılmaz, R., Mukherjee, K., Serra, M., & Anderson, J. (2025). The emergence and significance of meta-identity in the professional development of experienced teacher-researchers. *Teacher Development*, 1–20. https://doi.org/10.1080/13664530.2025.2515916.

Dodman, S. L. (2021). Learning, leadership, and agency: A case study of teacher-initiated professional development. *Professional Development in Education, 48*(3), 398–410. https://doi.org/10.1080/19415257.2021.1955731.

Donmez, M. (2024). AI-based feedback tools in education: A comprehensive bibliometric analysis study. *International Journal of Assessment Tools in Education, 11*(4), 622–646. https://doi.org/10.21449/ijate.1467476.

Dovchin, S. (2020). Introduction to special issue: Linguistic racism. *International Journal of Bilingual Education and Bilingualism, 23*(7), 773–777. https://doi.org/10.1080/13670050.2020.1778630.

Dovchin, S. (2022). *Translingual discrimination*. Cambridge University Press.

Dovchin, S. (2025). Beyond linguistic racism: Linguicism and intersectionality among Mongolian background postgraduate female students in Australia. *Urban Education*. https://doi.org/10.1177/00420859251331555.

Dovchin, S., & Marlina, R. (2025). Accent, access, and agency: A conversation with Professor Sender Dovchin on language and injustice. *RELC Journal*. https://doi.org/10.1177/00336882251351112.

Dovchin, S., Wang, M., & Steele, C. (2025). Translingual entanglements of emotions and translanguaging in language learning and teaching contexts. *International Journal of Applied Linguistics*, *35*(3), 987–995. https://doi.org/10.1111/ijal.12690.

Ellsworth, E. (1989). Why doesn't this feel empowering? Working through the repressive myths of critical pedagogy. *Harvard Educational Review*, *59*(3), 297–324. https://doi.org/10.17763/haer.59.3.058342114k266250.

Emeagwali, G., George, J., & Dei, S. (Eds.) (2014). *African indigenous knowledge and the disciplines*. SensePublishers.

Fairclough, N. (1995). *Critical discourse analysis: The critical study of language*. Longman.

Fairclough, N. (2003). *Analysing discourse* (Vol. 270). Routledge.

Fairclough, N. (2013). *Language and power*. Routledge.

Fairley, M. J. (2025). A Case for teacher inquiry groups for exploring language teacher identity constructions in transnational contexts. *RELC Journal*, *56*(1), 16–33. https://doi.org/10.1177/00336882241313389.

Fallas-Escobar, C., & Herrera, L. J. P. (2022). Examining raciolinguistic struggles in institutional settings: A duoethnography. *Linguistics and Education*, *67*, 101012. https://doi.org/10.1016/j.linged.2022.101012.

Fang, F., Zhang, L. J., & Sah, P. K. (2022). Translanguaging in language teaching and learning: Current practices and future directions. *RELC Journal*, *53*(2), 305–312. https://doi.org/10.1177/00336882221114478.

Farrell, T. S., & Farrell, A. H. (2025). Reflective practice in language teacher education: A systematic review. In Z. Tajeddin & T. S. C. Farrell (Eds.), *Handbook of language teacher education: critical review and research synthesis* (pp. 3–34). Springer Nature Switzerland. https://doi.org/10.1007/978-3-031-47310-4_2.

Firth, A., & Wagner, J. (1997). On discourse, communication, and (some) fundamental concepts in SLA research. *The Modern Language Journal*, *81*(3), 285–300. https://doi.org/10.1111/j.1540-4781.1997.tb05480.x.

Fitzclarence, L., & Giroux, H. A. (1984). The paradox of power in educational theory and practice. *Language Arts*, *61*(5), 462–477. https://doi.org/10.58680/la198425970.

Fitzgerald, T., & Hall, D. (2021). Performativity, managerialism, and educational leadership. In S. J. Courtney, H. M. Gunter, R. Niesche, & T. Trujillo (Eds.), *Understanding educational leadership: Critical perspectives and approaches* (pp. 323–338). Bloomsbury.

Forrest, M. (2013). Practising silence in teaching. *Journal of Philosophy of Education*, *47*(4), 605–622. https://doi.org/10.1111/1467-9752.12043.

Foucault, M. (1979). *Discipline and punish: The birth of the prison* (A. Sheridan, Trans.). Random House. (Original work published 1975).

Foucault, M. (1980). *Power/Knowledge: Selected interviews and other writings, 1972–1977* (C. Gordon, Ed. & Trans.). Pantheon Books.

Freed, A. F. (2015). Institutional discourse. In K. Tracy, C. Ilie, & T. Sandel (Eds.), *The international encyclopedia of language and social interaction*. Wiley. https://doi.org/10.1002/9781118611463.wbielsi151.

Freedman, M. (2007). *Teacher education and the struggle for social justice*. Routledge.

Freeman, D., & Johnson, K. E. (1998). Reconceptualizing the knowledge-base of language teacher education. *TESOL Quarterly*, *32*(3), 397–417. https://doi.org/10.2307/3588114.

Freire, P. (2000). *Pedagogy of the oppressed* (M. B. Ramos, Trans.; 30th anniversary ed.). Continuum (Original work published 1970).

Gallien, C. (2020). A decolonial turn in the humanities [في للاستعمار المقوّض المنعطف الإنــســانــيــات]. *Alif: Journal of Comparative Poetics*, *40*(1), 28–58. https://doi.org/10.1163/3050760X-04001004.

García, O. (2009). *Bilingual education in the 21st century: A global perspective*. Wiley/Blackwell.

Garsten, C., & Jacobsson, K. (2013). Post-political regulation: Soft power and post-political visions in global governance. *Critical Sociology*, *39*(3), 421–437. https://doi.org/10.1177/0896920511413942.

Gee, J. P. (2000). Identity as an analytic lens for research in education. *Review of Research in Education*, *25*(1), 99–125. https://doi.org/10.3102/0091732X025001099.

Gilmore, P. (1985). Silence and sulking: Emotional displays in the classroom. In D. Tannen & M. Saville-Troike (Eds.), *Perspectives on silence* (pp. 139–162). Norwood, NJ: Ablex.

Giroux, H. A. (2020). *On critical pedagogy* (2nd ed.). Bloomsbury Academic.

Good, A. G. (2018). *Teachers at the table: Voice, agency, and advocacy in educational policymaking*. Bloomsbury.

Graham, S. S., & Hopkins, H. R. (2021). AI for social justice: New methodological horizons in technical communication. *Technical Communication Quarterly*, *31*(1), 89–102. https://doi.org/10.1080/10572252.2021.1955151.

Gray, J., & Block, D. (2013). The marketisation of language teacher education and neoliberalism: Characteristics, consequences and future prospects. In D. Block, J. Gray, & M. Holborow (Eds.), *Neoliberalism and applied linguistics* (pp. 114–143). Routledge.

Groothuijsen, S. E. A., Bronkhorst, L. H., Prins, G. T., & Kuiper, W. (2019). Teacher-researchers' quality concerns for practice-oriented educational research. *Research Papers in Education, 35*(6), 766–787. https://doi.org/10.1080/02671522.2019.1633558.

Harmon, M. R., & Wilson, M. J. (2012). *Beyond grammar: Language, power, and the classroom: Resources for teachers*. Routledge.

Hartnett, A., & Naish, M. (1993). Democracy, teachers and the struggle for education: An essay in the political economy of teacher education. *Curriculum Studies, 1*(3), 335–348. https://doi.org/10.1080/0965975930010303.

Harumi, S. (2011). Classroom silence: Voices from Japanese EFL learners. *ELT Journal, 65*(3), 260–269. https://doi.org/10.1093/elt/ccq046.

Harvey, D. (2005). *A brief history of neoliberalism*. Oxford University Press.

Hawkins, M., & Norton, B. (2009). Critical language teacher education. In A. Burns & J. C. Richards (Eds.), *The Cambridge guide to second language teacher education* (pp. 30–39). Cambridge University Press.

Heller, M., & Martin-Jones, M. (2001). Introduction: Symbolic domination, education, and linguistic difference. In M. Heller & M. Martin-Jones (Eds.), *Voices of authority: Education and linguistic difference* (pp. 1–28). Ablex.

Heron, M., Donaghue, H., & Balloo, K. (2023). Observational feedback literacy: Designing post observation feedback for learning. *Teaching in Higher Education, 29*(8), 2061–2074. https://doi.org/10.1080/13562517.2023.2191786.

Hilferty, F. (2008). Theorising teacher professionalism as an enacted discourse of power. *British Journal of Sociology of Education, 29*(2), 161–173. https://doi.org/10.1080/01425690701837521.

Hiratsuka, T., Nall, M., & Castellano, J. (2024). Trans-speakerism: A trioethnographic exploration into diversity, equity, and inclusion in language education. *Language and Education, 38*(6), 1044–1060. https://doi.org/10.1080/09500782.2023.2223565.

Hobbs, V. (2013). "A basic starter pack": The TESOL Certificate as a course in survival. *ELT Journal, 67*(2), 163–174. https://doi.org/10.1093/elt/ccs078.

Hofer, B., & Jessner, U. (2025). Research agenda: From monolingual to multilingual norms in multilingual classrooms. *Language Teaching*, 1–16. https://doi.org/10.1017/S0261444825000023.

Holden, G. (2002). Towards a Learning Community: The role of mentoring in teacher-led school improvement. *Journal of In-Service Education, 28*(1), 9–22. https://doi.org/10.1080/13674580200200168.

Holliday, A. (2005). *The struggle to teach English as an international language*. Oxford University Press.

Holliday, A. (2006). Native-speakerism. *ELT Journal, 60*(4), 385–387. https://doi.org/10.1093/elt/ccl030.

Holliday, A. (2015). Native-speakerism: Taking the concept forward and achieving cultural belief. In A. Swan, P. Aboshiha, & A. Holliday (Eds.), *(En)countering native-speakerism: Global perspectives* (pp. 11–25). Palgrave Advances in Languages & Linguistics.

Holliday, A. (2018). *Understanding intercultural communication: Negotiating a grammar of culture*. Routledge.

Holliday, A. (2021). Linguaculture, cultural travel, native-speakerism and small culture formation on the go. In R. Rubbi, R. Tuppas, & M. Saraceni (Eds.), *Bloomsbury world Englishes volume 2: Ideologies* (pp. 101–112). Bloomsbury.

Holliday, A. (2022). *Contesting grand narratives of the intercultural*. Routledge.

Holmes, J. (2006). Sharing a laugh: Pragmatic aspects of humor and gender in the workplace. *Journal of Pragmatics, 38*(1), 26–50. https://doi.org/10.1016/j.pragma.2005.06.007.

Holmes, J. & Marra, M. (2002). Over the edge? Subversive humor between colleagues and friends. *Humor, 15*(1), 65–87. https://doi.org/10.1515/humr.2002.006.

Holzscheiter, A. (2005). Discourse as capability: Non-state actors' capital in global governance. *Millennium, 33*(3), 723–746. https://doi.org/10.1177/03058298050330030301.

Hornstein, J., Keller, M. V., Greisel, M., Dresel, M., & Kollar, I. (2025). Enhancing the peer-feedback process through instructional support: A meta-analysis. *Educational Psychology Review, 37*(2), 42. https://doi.org/10.1007/s10648-025-10017-3.

Houghton, S. A., & Bouchard, J. (eds.) (2020). *Native-speakerism: Its resilience and undoing*. Springer.

Houghton, S. A., & Rivers, D. J. (eds.) (2013). *Native-speakerism in Japan: Intergroup dynamics in foreign language education*. Multilingual Matters.

Hudson, A. K., & Pletcher, B. C. (2020). The art of asking questions: Unlocking the power of a coach's language. *The Reading Teacher, 74*(1), 96–100. https://doi.org/10.1002/trtr.1911.

Humonen, K., & Whittle, A. (2025). "Just relax and ram it in": Dimensions of power in workplace sexual humour. *Organization, 32*(3), 345–376. https://doi.org/10.1177/13505084231201277.

Hunt, C. S. (2018). Toward dialogic professional learning: Negotiating authoritative discourses within literacy coaching interaction. *Research in the Teaching of English, 52*(3), 262–287.

Jary, D. (2013). Aspects of the "Audit Society": Issues arising from the colonization of professional academic identities by a "portable management tool." In M. Dent & S. Whitehead, *Managing professional identities* (pp. 38–60). Routledge.

Javahery, P., & Kamali, J. (2023). Teachers' personality types and their attitude toward receiving and employing postobservation feedback. *Psychology in the Schools, 60*(8), 3073–3089. https://doi.org/10.1002/pits.22900.

Jaworski, A. (1992). *The power of silence: Social and pragmatic perspectives*. Sage.

Jaworski, A., & Sachdev, I. (1998). Beliefs about silence in the classroom. *Language and Education, 12*(4), 273–292. https://doi.org/10.1080/09500789808666754.

Jhagroe, S., & Salazar-Morales, D. (2025). A theory of policy coloniality: The role of race and colonial knowledge in policy formulation. *Critical Policy Studies*, 1–21. https://doi.org/10.1080/19460171.2025.2533758.

Johnson, K. E. (2016). Language teacher education. In G. Hall (Eds.), *The Routledge handbook of English language teaching* (pp. 121–134). Routledge.

Johnson, K. E., & Golombek, P. R. (2020). Informing and transforming language teacher education pedagogy. *Language Teaching Research, 24*(1), 116–127. https://doi.org/10.1177/1362168818777539.

Kachru, B. B. (1986). *The alchemy of English: The spread functions and models of non-native Englishes*. Pergamon.

Kamali, J. (2014). Post method survival. *Procedia-Social and Behavioral Sciences, 98*, 824–829. https://doi.org/10.1016/j.sbspro.2014.03.487.

Kamali, J. (2024). A cross-cultural investigation of effective language pedagogy in teachers' personal practical knowledge narratives: A cultural-ecological perspective. *Pedagogy, Culture & Society, 33*(3), 1089–1109. https://doi.org/10.1080/14681366.2024.2361455.

Kamali, J. (2025). Revisiting an Anti-Machiavellian model for teacher education: A critical perspective. *Power and Education, 17*(1), 96–112. https://doi.org/10.1177/17577438231225157.

Kamali, J., & Alpat, M. F. (2025). "... Like white light going through a prism": a metaphorical exploration of multilingual education from teachers' perspectives. *International Journal of Multilingualism*, 1–20. https://doi.org/10.1080/14790718.2025.2456061.

Kamali, J. & Anderson, J. (2025). Narrative self-observation: A new framework for teacher professional development and identity research. *European Journal of Teacher Education*. https://doi.org/10.1080/02619768.2025.2563113.

Kamali, J., & Javahery, P. (2024). Examining the interplay of Teacher emotional intelligence and feedback responsiveness in post-observation conferences: Voices from Iran. *Human Arenas*, 1–23. https://doi.org/10.1007/s42087-024-00438-x.

Kamali, J., & Javahery, P. (2025). Collaborative reflection as a means to improve teachers' reflective skills: A community of practice perspective. *Reflective Practice*, *26*(2), 246–261. https://doi.org/10.1080/14623943.2024.2426279.

Kamali, J., & Nazari, M. (2025). Transnational language teachers' emotional vulnerability and professional identity construction: an ecological perspective. *Journal of Multilingual and Multicultural Development*, *46*(7), 1857–1871. https://doi.org/10.1080/01434632.2023.2257659.

Kamali, J., Javahery, P., Zendehbad, M., Shahraki, M., & Rasouli, M. (2025). A sociocultural exploration of Iranian language teachers' corrective feedback: Why and how? *Cambridge Journal of Education*, *55*(1), 73–91. https://doi.org/10.1080/0305764X.2025.2451261.

Kayi-Aydar, H. (2019). Language teacher identity. *Language Teaching*, *52*(3), 281–295. https://doi.org/10.1017/S0261444819000223.

Kim, M. Y., & Wilkinson, I. A. (2019). What is dialogic teaching? Constructing, deconstructing, and reconstructing a pedagogy of classroom talk. *Learning, Culture and Social Interaction*, *21*, 70–86. https://doi.org/10.1016/j.lcsi.2019.02.003.

Koay, J. (2023). Self-directed professional development activities: An autoethnography. *Teaching and Teacher Education*, *133*, 104258. https://doi.org/10.1016/j.tate.2023.104258.

Korthagen, F. (2004). In search of the essence of a good teacher: Towards a more holistic approach in teacher education. *Teaching and Teacher Education*, *20*(1), 77–97. https://doi.org/10.1016/j.tate.2003.10.002.

Korthagen, F. (2017). Inconvenient truths about teacher learning: Towards professional development 3.0. *Teachers and Teaching*, *23*(4), 387–405. https://doi.org/10.1080/13540602.2016.1211523.

Kramsch, C. (Ed.). (2003). *Language acquisition and language socialization: Ecological perspectives*. Bloomsbury.

Kubota, R. (1999). Japanese culture constructed by discourses: Implications for applied linguistics research and ELT. *TESOL Quarterly*, *33*(1), 9–35. https://doi.org/10.2307/3588189.

Kubota, R. (2009). Rethinking the superiority of the native speaker: Toward a relational understanding of power. In R. Kumaravadivelu (Ed.), *The Cambridge guide to second language teacher education* (pp. 115–122). Cambridge University Press.

Kubota, R. (2023). Foreword. In P. K. Sah & F. Fang (Eds.), *Policies, politics, and ideologies of English-medium instruction in Asian universities: Unsettling critical edges* (pp. vii–x). Routledge.

Kumar, A. (2018). *Curriculum in international contexts: Understanding colonial, ideological, and neoliberal influences*. Springer.

Kumaravadivelu, B. (1994). The postmethod condition:(E) merging strategies for second/foreign language teaching. *TESOL Quarterly, 28*(1), 27–48. https://doi.org/10.2307/3587197.

Kumaravadivelu, B. (2012). *Language teacher education for a global society: A modular model for knowing, analyzing, recognizing, doing, and seeing*. Routledge.

Kupolati, O. O. (2024). Beyond home language: Heritage language maintenance practices of Yorùbá–English bilingual immigrants. *International Journal of Bilingualism, 28*(3), 570–590. https://doi.org/10.1177/13670069231175266.

Kuzu, T. E., Irion, T., & Bay, W. (2025). AI-based task development in teacher education: an empirical study on using ChatGPT to create complex multilingual tasks in the context of primary education. *Education and Information Technologies*, 30, 23041–23075. https://doi.org/10.1007/s10639-025-13673-8.

Lippi-Green, R. (1997). *English with an accent: Language ideology and discrimination in the United States*. Routledge.

Llurda, E., & Calvet-Terré, J. (2025). Language teacher nativeness/nonnativeness: A systematic review. In Z. Tajeddin & T. S. C. Farrell (Eds.), *Handbook of language teacher education: Critical review and research synthesis* (pp. 1–25). Springer Nature Switzerland. https://doi.org/10.1007/978-3-031-43208-8_5-1.

Lodge, R. A. (2004). *A sociolinguistic history of Parisian French*. Cambridge University Press.

Lowe, R. J. (2020). *Uncovering ideology in English language teaching: Identifying the "native speaker" frame*. Springer.

Macaulay, C. D. (2025). Power asymmetries in inter-organizational relationships: A case study using institutionalism. *Sport, Business and Management: An International Journal, 15*(2), 140–160. https://doi.org/10.1108/SBM-07-2024-0092.

Macedo, D. (2019). Rupturing the yoke of colonialism in foreign language education: An introduction. In D. Macedo (Eds.), *Decolonizing foreign language education* (pp. 1–49). Routledge.

Macias, A. (2017). Teacher-led professional development: A proposal for a bottom-up structure approach. *International Journal of Teacher Leadership, 8*(1), 76–91.

Mackenzie, L. (2021). Discriminatory job advertisements for English language teachers in Colombia: An analysis of recruitment biases. *TESOL Journal, 12* (1), 1–21. https://doi.org/10.1002/tesj.535.

Malderez, A. (2003). Observation. *ELT Journal, 57*(2), 179–181. https://doi.org/10.1093/elt/57.2.179.

Maldonado-Torres, N. (2007). On the coloniality of being: Contributions to the development of a concept1. *Cultural Studies, 21*(2–3), 240–270. https://doi.org/10.1080/09502380601162548.

Mann, S., & Walsh, S. (2017). *Reflective practice in English language teaching: Research-based principles and practices*. Routledge.

Marginson, S. (2016). The worldwide trend to high participation higher education: Dynamics of social stratification in inclusive systems. *Higher Education, 72*, 413–434. https://doi.org/10.1007/s10734-016-0016-x.

Marlina, R., & Giri, R. A. (Eds.). (2014). *The pedagogy of English as an international language: Perspectives from scholars, teachers, and students*. Springer.

Martín Rojo, L. (2010). *Constructing inequality in multilingual classrooms*. Mouton de Gruyter.

Martin, P. (2005). 'Safe' language practices in two rural schools in Malaysia: Tensions between policy and practice. In A. M. Y. Lin & P. W. Martin (Eds.), *Decolonisation, globalisation: Language-in-education policy and practice* (pp. 74–97). Multilingual Matters.

May, S. (Ed.). (2014). *The multilingual turn: Implications for SLA, TESOL and bilingual education*. Routledge.

McKinney, C. (2016). *Language and power in post-colonial schooling: Ideologies in practice*. Routledge.

McLaren, H. J. (2016). Silence as a power. *Social Alternatives, 35*(1), 3–5.

McLaughlin, A., Walls, J. H., & Kruse, S. (2025). Principal discipline decision-making: Choices and challenges. *Educational Management Administration & Leadership*. https://doi.org/10.1177/17411432251330958.

McMain, E. (2023). Getting good at bad emotion: Teachers resist and reproduce hegemonic positivity in a discourse community. *Critical Studies in Education, 65*(1), 57–74. https://doi.org/10.1080/17508487.2023.2217867.

Meddings, L., & Thornbury, S. (2009). *Teaching unplugged: Dogme in English language teaching*. Delta.

Mehan, H. (1979). *Learning lessons: Social organization in the classroom*. Harvard University Press.

Meier, G. S. (2017). The multilingual turn as a critical movement in education: Assumptions, challenges and a need for reflection. *Applied Linguistics Review, 8*(1), 131–161. https://doi.org/10.1515/applirev-2016-2010.

Meighan, P. J. (2022). *Colonialingualism*: Colonial legacies, imperial mindsets, and inequitable practices in English language education. *Diaspora, Indigenous, and Minority Education*, *17*(2), 146–155. https://doi.org/10.1080/15595692.2022.2082406.

Meighan, P. J. (2025). Transepistemic language teacher education: A framework for plurilingualism, translanguaging, and challenging colonialingualism. *The Modern Language Journal*. *109*(3), 651–670. https://doi.org/10.1111/modl.13020.

Mercer, N. (2000). *Words and minds: How we use language to think together*. Routledge.

Mignolo, W. (2012). Decolonizing Western epistemology/building decolonial epistemologies. In A. M. Isasi-Díaz & E. Mendieta (Eds.), *Decolonizing epistemologies: Latina/o theology and philosophy* (pp. 19–43). Fordham University Press. https://doi.org/10.5422/fordham/9780823241354.003.0002.

Mirhosseini, S. A. (2018). An invitation to the less-treaded path of autoethnography in TESOL research. *TESOL Journal*, *9*(1), 76–92. https://doi.org/10.1002/tesj.305.

Mockler, N. (2020). Teacher professional learning under audit: Reconfiguring practice in an age of standards. *Professional Development in Education*, *48*(1), 166–180. https://doi.org/10.1080/19415257.2020.1720779.

Mökkönen, A. C. (2012). Social organization through teacher-talk: Subteaching, socialization and the normative use of language in a multilingual primary class. *Linguistics and Education*, *23*(3), 310–322. https://doi.org/10.1016/j.linged.2012.06.001.

Moorhouse, B. L., & Kohnke, L. (2024). The effects of generative AI on initial language teacher education: The perceptions of teacher educators. *System*, *122*, 103290. https://doi.org/10.1016/j.system.2024.103290.

Moorhouse, B. L., Wan, Y., Wu, C. et al. (2024). Developing language teachers' professional generative AI competence: An intervention study in an initial language teacher education course. *System*, *125*, 103399. https://doi.org/10.1016/j.system.2024.103399.

Morgan, B. (1997). Identity and intonation: Linking dynamic processes in an ESL classroom. *TESOL Quarterly*, *31*(3), 431–450. https://doi.org/10.2307/3587833.

Mortimer, E., & Scott, P. (2003). *Meaning making in secondary science classrooms*. McGraw-Hill Education.

Nassaji, H. (2007). Elicitation and reformulation and their relationship with learner repair in dyadic interaction. *Language learning*, *57*(4), 511–548. https://doi.org/10.1111/j.1467-9922.2007.00427.x.

Nassaji, H., & Wells, G. (2000). What's the use of "triadic dialogue"? An investigation of teacher–student interaction. *Applied Linguistics*, *21*(3), 376–406. https://doi.org/10.1093/applin/21.3.376.

National Institute of Standards and Technology. (2023). *AI risk management framework (AI RMF 1.0)* (NIST Special Publication No. 1270). U.S. Department of Commerce. https://doi.org/10.6028/NIST.SP.1270.

Nazari, M. (2025). Making sense of Gee and identity in (language) teaching. *Language Teacher Education Research*, *2*, 1–10. https://doi.org/10.32038/lter.2025.02.01.

Neophytou, L. (2025). An alternative reading of the European Standards and Guidelines (ESG): From Foucault's panopticon to Freire's humanizing pedagogy. *Policy Futures in Education*, *23*(4), 783–808. https://doi.org/10.1177/14782103251320233.

Ning, Y., Zhang, C., Xu, B., Zhou, Y., & Wijaya, T. T. (2024). Teachers' AI-TPACK: Exploring the relationship between knowledge elements. *Sustainability*, *16*(3), 978. https://doi.org/10.3390/su16030978.

Northedge, A. (2003). Rethinking Teaching in the Context of Diversity. *Teaching in Higher Education*, *8*(1), 17–32. https://doi.org/10.1080/1356251032000052302.

Norton, B. (1997). Language, identity, and the ownership of English. *TESOL Quarterly*, *31*(3), 409–429. https://doi.org/10.2307/3587831.

Nunan, D., & Choi, J. (2010). *Language and culture: Reflective narratives and the emergence of identity*. Routledge.

Nystrand, M. (1997). *Opening dialogue: Understanding the dynamics of language and learning in the English classroom*. Teachers College Press.

O'Leary, M. (2013). Surveillance, performativity and normalised practice: The use and impact of graded lesson observations in Further Education colleges. *Journal of Further and Higher Education*, *37*(5), 694–714. https://doi.org/10.1080/0309877X.2012.684036.

O'Leary, M. (2020). *Classroom observation: A guide to the effective observation of teaching and learning* (2nd ed.). Routledge.

Paechter, C. (2000). Power, gender and curriculum. In C. Paechter, M. Preedy, D. Scott, & J. Soler (Eds.), *Knowledge, power and learning* (pp. 1–6). Paul Chapman.

Paikeday, T. (1985). *The native speaker is dead!*. Paikeday.

Pallas, A. M., & Touloukian, C. (2024). A taxonomy of subjective control: Teachers' narrative accounts of a teacher evaluation system. *Teachers College Record*, *126*(2), 26–69. https://doi.org/10.1177/01614681241240283.

Patel, M., Solly, M., & Copeland, S. (2023). *The future of English: Global perspectives*. British Council. www.britishcouncil.org/future-of-english.

Peal, E., & Lambert, W. E. (1962). The relation of bilingualism to intelligence. *Psychological Monographs: General and Applied, 76*(27), 1–23. https://doi.org/10.1037/h0093840.

Pennington, M. C., & Richards, J. C. (2016). Teacher identity in language teaching: Integrating personal, contextual, and professional factors. *RELC Journal, 47*(1), 5–23. https://doi.org/10.1177/0033688216631219.

Pennycook, A. (2001). *Critical applied linguistics: A critical introduction.* Mahwah, NJ: Lawrence Erlbaum Associates.

Pennycook, A. (2021). *Critical applied linguistics: A critical re-introduction.* Routledge.

Pentón Herrera, L. J. (2022). Is the language you teach racist?: Reflections and considerations for English and Spanish (teacher) educators. *International Journal of Literacy, Culture, and Language Education, 2*, 58–70. https://doi.org/10.14434/ijlcle.v2iMay.34390.

Pentón Herrera, L. J. (2024). An agenda for emotional intelligence in language teacher education. *Language Teacher Education Research, 1*, 48–63. https://doi.org/10.32038/lter.2024.01.03.

Pentón Herrera, L. J., & Martínez-Alba, G. (2022). Emotions, well-being, and language teacher identity development in an EFL teacher preparation program. *Korea TESOL Journal, 18*(1), 1–25.

Peter, L. J., & Hull, R. (1969). *The peter principle* (Vol. 4). Souvenir Press.

Phillipson, R. (1992). *Linguistic imperialism.* Oxford University Press.

Phillipson, R. (2013). *Linguistic imperialism continued.* Routledge.

Plato. (2004). *Gorgias* (W. C. Helmbold, Trans.). In E. Hamilton & H. Cairns (Eds.), *The collected dialogues of Plato* (pp. 229–307). Princeton University Press. (Original work ca. 380 BCE)

Plester, B. (2016). *The complexity of workplace humour: Laughter, jokers and the dark side of humour.* Springer.

Poehner, M. E., & Lantolf, J. P. (2024). *Sociocultural theory and second language developmental education.* Cambridge University Press.

Prabhu, N. S. (1990). There is no best method – Why?. *TESOL Quarterly, 24*(2), 161–176. https://doi.org/10.2307/3586897.

Priestley, M., Biesta, G., & Robinson, S. (2015). *Teacher agency: An ecological approach.* Bloomsbury Academic.

Rampton, M. B. H. (1990). Displacing the "native speaker": Expertise, affiliation, and inheritance. *ELT Journal, 44*(2), 97–101. https://doi.org/10.1093/eltj/44.2.97.

Resnick, L. B. (1999). Making America smarter. *Education Week*, 18(40), 38–40.

Rivers, D. J. (2018). The idea of the native speaker. In S. A. Houghton, D. J. Rivers, & K. Hashimoto (Eds.), *Beyond native-speakerism: Current explorations and future visions* (pp. 15–35). Routledge.

Rumi, J. (n.d.). *Divan-e Shams-e Tabrizi, Ghazal 1197*. Ganjoor. Retrieved August 17, 2025, from https://ganjoor.net/.

Rubin, J. C., & Tily, S. (2021). Beginning teachers in early childhood education: A critical discourse analysis of policies in Aotearoa New Zealand and the United States. *Policy Futures in Education*, *19*(4), 438–458. https://doi.org/10.1177/14782103211001638.

Ruecker, T., & Ives, L. (2015). White native English speakers needed: The rhetorical construction of privilege in online teacher recruitment spaces. *TESOL Quarterly*, *49*(4), 733–756. https://doi.org/10.1002/tesq.195

Sah, P. K., & Fang, F. (2025). Decolonizing English-medium instruction in the global south. *TESOL Quarterly*, *59*(1), 565–579. https://doi.org/10.1002/tesq.3307.

Salton, Y. A. (2019). *Images of the teacher self in an era of teacher quality and standardisation* (Doctoral dissertation, University of Southern Queensland).

Sedova, K., & Navratilova, J. (2020). Silent students and the patterns of their participation in classroom talk. *Journal of the Learning Sciences*, *29*(4–5), 681–716. https://doi.org/10.1080/10508406.2020.1794878.

Seedhouse, P. (2004). The interactional architecture of the language classroom: A conversation analysis perspective. *Language Learning*, *54*(Suppl1), x–300. https://doi.org/10.1111/j.1467-9922.2004.00266.x.

Seidlhofer, B., Breiteneder, A., & Pitzl, M. L. (2006). English as a lingua franca in Europe: Challenges for applied linguistics. *Annual Review of Applied Linguistics*, *26*, 3–34. https://doi.org/10.1017/S026719050600002X.

Seidman, S., & Alexander, J. C. (2020). Power/knowledge. In S. Seidman & J. C. Alexander (Eds.), *The new social theory reader* (pp. 73–79). Routledge.

Selvi, A. F. (2014). Myths and misconceptions about nonnative English speakers in the TESOL (NNEST) movement. *TESOL Journal*, *5*(3), 573–611. https://doi.org/10.1002/tesj.158.

Selvi, A. F., Yazan, B., & Mahboob, A. (2024). Research on "native" and "non-native" English-speaking teachers: Past developments, current status, and future directions. *Language Teaching*, *57*(1), 1–41. https://doi.org/10.1017/S0261444823000137.

Shor, I., & Freire, P. (1987). What is the "dialogical method" of teaching?. *Journal of Education*, *169*(3), 11–31. https://doi.org/10.1177/002205748716900303.

Shore, C., & Wright, S. (2015). Audit culture revisited: Rankings, ratings, and the reassembling of society. *Current Anthropology, 56*(3), 421–444. https://doi.org/10.1086/681534.

Sinclair, J. M., & Coulthard, M. (1975). *Towards an analysis of discourse: The English used by teachers and pupils.* Oxford University Press.

Skourdoumbis, A., & Madkur, A. (2020). Symbolic capital and the problem of navigating English language teacher practice: The case of Indonesian pesantren. *TESOL in Context, 29*(2), 15–34.

Sorensen, M. J. (2008). Humor as a serious strategy of nonviolent resistance to oppression. *Peace & Change, 33*(2), 167–190. https://doi.org/10.1111/j.1468-0130.2008.00488.x.

Sperti, S. (2025). Multilingualism, multiculturalism and language teaching: Insights into teachers' challenges and needs from continuous professional development. In S. Karpava (Ed.), *Multilingualism and multiculturalism in Language education* (pp. 277–302). Springer Nature Switzerland.

Stoll, L., Bolam, R., McMahon, A., Wallace, M., & Thomas, S. (2006). Professional learning communities: A review of the literature. *Journal of Educational Change, 7*(4), 221–258. https://doi.org/10.1007/s10833-006-0001-8.

Stoll, L., Brown, C., Spence-Thomas, K., & Taylor, C. (2017). Teacher leadership within and across professional learning communities. In A. Harris, M. Jones, & J. B. Huffman (Eds.), *Teachers leading educational reform* (pp. 51–71). Routledge.

Swan, A., Aboshiha, P., & Holliday, A. (eds.) (2015). *(En)Countering native-speakerism: Global perspectives.* Palgrave Macmillan.

Swargiary, K. (2024). *How AI revolutionizes regional language education.* Scholar Press.

Sweeting, A. M., & Carey, M. D. (2025). Strengthening the nexus of research and practice in CELTA pronunciation instruction. *System, 130,* 103623. https://doi.org/10.1016/j.system.2025.103623.

Szymborska, W. (1995). *Children of our age* (S. Baranczak & C. Cavanagh, Trans.). In *View with a grain of sand: Selected poems* (pp. 149–120). Harcourt Brace.

Tajeddin, Z., & Kamali, J. (2020). Typology of scaffolding in teacher discourse: Large data-based evidence from second language classrooms. *International Journal of Applied Linguistics, 30*(2), 329–343. https://doi.org/10.1111/ijal.12286.

Tajeddin, Z., & Kamali, J. (2023). Teachers' classroom interactional competence: Scale development and validation. *Language Teaching Research Quarterly, 35,* 1–20. https://doi.org/10.32038/ltrq.2023.35.01.

Tajeddin, Z., & Yazan, B. (Eds.). (2024). *Language teacher identity tensions: Nexus of agency, emotion, and investment*. Taylor & Francis.

Tan, K. H. (2012). How teachers understand and use power in alternative assessment. *Education Research International*, *2012*(1), 382465. https://doi.org/10.1155/2012/382465.

Tan, S. C., Tan, A. L., & Lee, A. V. Y. (2024). Breaking the silence: Understanding teachers' use of silence in classrooms. *Pedagogies: An International Journal*, *20*(3), 331–348. https://doi.org/10.1080/1554480X.2024.2341258.

Thornborrow, J. (2014). *Power talk: Language and interaction in institutional discourse*. Routledge.

Towler, M. A. (2025). Language variation on Arabic undergraduate degree courses in England: Students' perspectives. *The Language Learning Journal*, *53*(2), 173–200. https://doi.org/10.1080/09571736.2024.2351938.

Turner, M., & Lin, A. M. (2024). Translanguaging: Process and power in education. *Linguistics and Education*, *83*, 101340. https://doi.org/10.1016/j.linged.2024.101340.

Ushioda, E. (2017). The impact of global English on motivation to learn other languages: Toward an ideal multilingual self. *Modern Language Journal*, *101*(3), 469–482. https://doi.org/10.1111/modl.12413.

Uysal, H., & Sah, P. K. (2024). Language ideologies and language teaching in the global world: An introduction to the special issue. *International Journal of Bilingualism*, *28*(4), 611–617. https://doi.org/10.1177/13670069241240964.

van Lier, L. (Ed.). (2004). *The ecology and semiotics of language learning: A sociocultural perspective*. Springer Netherlands.

Vásquez, C. (2011). TESOL, teacher identity, and the need for "small story" research. *Tesol Quarterly*, *45*(3), 535–545. https://doi.org/10.5054/tq.2011.256800.

Wallace, M. J. (1991). *Training foreign language teachers*. Cambridge University Press.

Walsh, P. (2019). Precarity. *ELT Journal*, *73*(4), 459–462. https://doi.org/10.1093/elt/ccz029.

Walsh, S. (2011). *Exploring classroom discourse: Language in action*. Routledge.

Wang, T., Deng, M., & Tian, G. (2022). More leadership, more efficacy for inclusive practices? Exploring the relationships between distributed leadership, teacher leadership, and self-efficacy among inclusive education teachers in China. *Sustainability*, *14*(23), 16168. https://doi.org/10.3390/su142316168.

Watson, K. (1992). Language, education and political power: Some reflections on north-south relationships. *Language and Education*, *6*(2–4), 99–121. https://doi.org/10.1080/09500789209541331.

Watts, J. (2007). Can't take a joke? Humour as resistance, refuge and exclusion in a highly gendered workplace. *Feminism & Psychology, 17*(2), 259–66. https://doi.org/10.1177/0959353507076560.

Weber, M. (1968). *On charisma and institution building: Selected writings* (Vol. 322). University of Chicago Press.

Wegerif, R. (2011). Towards a dialogic theory of how children learn to think. *Thinking Skills and Creativity, 6*(3), 179–190. https://doi.org/10.1016/j.tsc.2011.08.002.

Wei, L., & Lin, A. M. Y. (2019). Translanguaging classroom discourse: pushing limits, breaking boundaries. *Classroom Discourse, 10*(3–4), 209–215. https://doi.org/10.1080/19463014.2019.1635032.

Wells, G. (1993). Reevaluating the IRF sequence: A proposal for the articulation of theories of activity and discourse for the analysis of teaching and learning in the classroom. *Linguistics and Education, 5*(1), 1–37. https://doi.org/10.1016/S0898-5898(05)80001-4.

Wells, G. (1999). *Dialogic inquiry: Toward a sociocultural practice and theory of education*. Cambridge University Press.

Wodak, R. (2012). Language, power and identity. *Language Teaching, 45*(2), 215–233. https://doi.org/10.1017/S0261444811000048.

Woodward, T. (2003). Loop input. *ELT Journal, 57*(3), 301–304. https://doi.org/10.1093/elt/57.3.301.

Woolard, K. A. (2020). *Language ideology*. In J. Stanlaw (Ed.), *The international encyclopedia of linguistic anthropology* (pp. 1–21). Wiley. https://doi.org/10.1002/9781118786093.iela0217.

Yazan, B. (2024). *Autoethnography in language education*. Palgrave Macmillan. https://doi.org/10.1007/978-3-031-57464-1_1.

Yilmaz, G. K. (2021). Translanguaging pedagogy and teacher agency in English language teaching: A systematic review. *Linguistics and Education, 62*, 100925. https://doi.org/10.1016/j.linged.2021.100925.

Zagzebski, L. T. (2012). *Epistemic authority: A theory of trust, authority, and autonomy in belief*. Oxford University Press.

Cambridge Elements

Language and Power

Luis Javier Pentón Herrera
VIZJA University

Luis Javier Pentón Herrera, Ph.D., D.Litt. (Hab.) is an award-winning Spanish and English educator and a best-selling author. In 2024, he was selected as the 2024 TESOL Teacher of the Year, awarded by the TESOL International Association and National Geographic Learning. He is a Professor (*Profesor uczelni*, in Polish) at Uniwersytet VIZJA, Poland. Originally from La Habana, Cuba, Luis Javier enjoys creative writing, playing with his two doggies, Virgo and Maui, and running.

Sender Dovchin
Curtin University

Sender Dovchin is a Professor and a Dean International at the Faculty of Humanities and Senior Principal Research Fellow at the School of Education, Curtin University, Australia. She is an Australian Research Council Fellow and Kakenhi Japan Society for the Promotion of Science Fellow. She is an Editor-in Chief of the *Critical Inquiry into Language Studies* journal. Her research advances second language education for migrant and Indigenous communities. She was named a Top Researcher in Language & Linguistics by *The Australian* (2021/2024/2025) research magazine and one of the Top 250 Researchers in Australia in 2021/2024/2025 respectively.

Editorial Board
Anna Becker, *Polish Academy of Sciences (Poland)*
Pramod K. Sah, *The Education University of Hong Kong (Hong Kong)*
Vander Tavares, *University of Inland Norway (Norway)*
Serafín M. Coronel-Molina, *Indiana University Bloomington (USA)*
Shaila Sultana, *BRAC University (Bangladesh)*
Annelies Kusters, *Heriot-Watt University (UK)*
Huseyin Uysal, *The Education University of Hong Kong (Hong Kong)*
Nashid Nigar, *Monash University (Australia)*
Michał Wilczewski, *Uniwersytet VIZJA (Poland)*
Ana Barcelos, *Universidade Federal de Viçosa (Brazil)*
Yasir Hussain, *Quaid-i-Azam University (Pakistan)*

About the Series
This Elements series explores the profound influence of language as a source of power and its role in shaping social dynamics. It examines how language can unite and divide, harm and heal, while also shaping perceptions, constructing realities, and influencing relationships within and across individuals, communities, and languages. Importantly, the series is interested in exploring the empowering and oppressive dimensions of language from various, interdisciplinary perspectives.

Cambridge Elements

Language and Power

Elements in the Series

Language as Power in the Language Teacher Education Ecosystem
Jaber Kamali

A full series listing is available at: www.cambridge.org/ELAP

For EU product safety concerns, contact us at Calle de José Abascal, 56–1°,
28003 Madrid, Spain or eugpsr@cambridge.org.

www.ingramcontent.com/pod-product-compliance
Ingram Content Group UK Ltd.
Pitfield, Milton Keynes, MK11 3LW, UK
UKHW022245220326
469255UK00019B/362